The Acquisition of th in Russia

SERIES

Vol. 1 THE ACQUISITION OF THE HOLY SPIRIT
  by I. M. Kontzevitch

Vol. 2 SALT OF THE EARTH: Elder Isidore
  by St. Paul Florensky

Vol. 3 ONE OF THE ANCIENTS: Elder Gabriel
  by St. Simeon Kholmogorov

Vol. 4 ELDER MELCHIZEDEK: Hermit of the Roslavl Forest
  by Serge N. Bolshakoff

Vol. 5 FATHER GERASIM OF NEW VALAAM
  by R. Monk Gerasim

ARCHIMANDRITE GERASIM

FATHER GERASIM
of New Valaam

by
R. MONK GERASIM (ELIEL)

*In commemoration of the 20th
Anniversary of Fr. Gerasim's repose*

NEW VALAAM MONASTERY • ALASKA
St. Herman Press
1989

†

Copyright 1989 by the
St. Herman of Alaska Brotherhood

Address all correspondence to:
St. Herman of Alaska Brotherhood
P. O. Box 70
Platina, California 96076
and
New Valaam Monastery
P. O. Box 90
Ouzinkie, Alaska 99644

FIRST EDITION

Cover: Archimandrite Gerasim on the path leading to the Sts. Sergius and Herman Church on Spruce Island, Alaska. From *National Geographic*, June, 1965.
Photograph by Wilbur E. Garrett. Copyright 1965 by the National Geographic Society.

Library of Congress Cataloging in Publication Data

Eliel, R. Monk Gerasim, 1961 -
  Father Gerasim of New Valaam.
    1. Christianity. 2. Russian Orthodox Church. 3. Alaska — Ecclesiastical History.
    I. Title.

Library of Congress Catalog Number 89-64024
ISBN 0-938635-29-8

CONTENTS

	Introduction	9
I.	The Life of Father Gerasim	11
II.	A Visit to Father Gerasim	49
III.	Desert Soliloquies on New Valaam: Random Treasures of Fr. Gerasim's Contemplations	55
IV.	Man's Heavenly Friends	85
V.	St. Tikhon of Kaluga and His Monastery	93
VI.	Is There Life Beyond the Grave?	99
	Epilogue: New Valaam Today	107

Fr. Gerasim on Spruce Island in 1938, age 50.

Introduction

THE SAINT HERMAN Brotherhood from its beginning has had three spiritual and ideologial benefactors who especially prayed and cared for its progress: Archbishop John Maximovitch (†1966), Prof. I. M. Kontzevitch (†1965), and Archimandrite Gerasim Schmaltz, who, on the eve of the Feast of the Protection of the Most Holy Theotokos in 1969, reposed into a better world, leaving us orphaned.

Long ago, when the Blessed Wonderworker of Alaska called Fr. Gerasim to serve him, Fr. Gerasim eagerly followed his call, only to discover what a lonely and hard path it was; and seeing how very few cared for a Saint of such great importance, he began to call through the press for the formation of a Brotherhood in the name of St. Herman, that the good name of America's Apostle of Orthodoxy become widely known. . . . But alas! his voice, although eloquent and truthful, was unheard for all these many, many years, until through the prayers of another holy man, Archbishop John Maximovitch, a humble beginning was laid in 1963, to the great joy of Fr. Gerasim, who blessed the brothers with an old metal icon found by him on Spruce Island, which, according to him, might very well have belonged to St. Herman. Giving his blessing, he wrote: "You are doing a good thing organizing a Brotherhood of Saint Herman, Wonderworker of Alaska! May God help you! But keep in mind that Satan does not like such things; he causes evil deeds to those who glorify God's chosen righteous people. I experienced myself the same thing upon my arrival in Alaska...."

Fr. Gerasim's constant prayers for us at the grave and relics of the Saint have been a living bond linking the Brotherhood to St. Herman. Therefore it is our duty, using his abundant correspondence to us, to speak the truth about Fr. Gerasim, sketching a brief, honest portrait of him and for the first time putting into proper perspective Fr. Gerasim's significance, which indeed constitutes a whole chapter of the *Life* of St. Herman.

We are publishing this book in commemoration of the 20th anniversary of Fr. Gerasim's repose. Trying to be faithful to the spiritual legacy he bequeathed to our Brotherhood, we want to keep alive his memory for the sake of those who care about holiness on the American soil. We view him not only as a local American phenomenon, but also as a man of God of universal significance, a suffering witness of Christ's righteousness in the 20th century.

The Monks of New Valaam
September 30/October 13, 1989

I

The Life of Father Gerasim

1. MONASTIC BEGINNINGS

Archimandrite Gerasim Schmaltz was born on October 28, 1888, in the Russian town of Alexin, Tula province, of pious Orthodox Russian parents, Alexander and Natalia. At baptism he was given the name Michael. From early childhood he was brought up on the Lives of Saints, in a strict church consciousness. Until his fifteenth year, although he had drunk in deeply the monastic spirit, he had not once been to a monastery. Here is how he describes his first visit to a monastery, from which is well evident the spiritual orientation which did not leave him to his death, and which guided his entire life.

"When I was fifteen years old, I came with Mother to the city of Tula, where I was to be sent to school. We stayed at the home of Mother's brother, my Uncle Nikolai Ivanovich Petrov, who then was living not far from [Shcheglov] monastery. . . . Strolling alone near Uncle's home, I longed with tears for my green forest back home, where I so loved to wander off and where I recalled all the great ascetics — monks who lived saving their souls in dense forests in the bosom of nature. . . . Once we were drinking tea at Uncle's in the garden and from this garden I saw golden crosses shining at sunset on dark blue domes, visible from behind the green trees. My heart leapt with joy when I heard that a holy place, for which my soul had longed since childhood, was so close.

FR. GERASIM'S NATIVE TOWN OF ALEXIN

On the back of this picture Fr. Gerasim wrote: "This photograph was received in 1934 from Russia. [It shows] a procession with the miracle-working icon of the Theotokos of Smolensk, which used to be brought every year from the village of Bundrevo to the town of Alexin — a distance of 7 versts — in the middle of the month of June. On the second day after its arrival it would be carried around town in a Cross procession. This photo was taken during that procession. The icon was still in a *riza* covering, which was massive, made of silver. This procession was instituted in memory of the deliverance from cholera and the black plague. In the photo is Fr. Lunev, a very good priest. Now the cathedral of Alexin is closed and Fr. Lunev is reduced to a pauper's existence. This is what our Orthodox Mother Russia has come to."

"On the next day, early in the morning, we went to the monastery. The weather was wonderful; the sun shone brightly from behind the birch grove that surrounded the monastery. At the gates of the holy monastery sat a monk, an old man, and I at once guessed that this was the gatekeeper, since I had already read many books on monasteries and the Lives of the Holy Fathers. . . . I wanted to see Elder Dometian and to open my soul to him and ask his blessing to leave the world for good and settle in the hermitage." He did not see the Elder then, but "in January, 1906, I traveled to the Elder for his blessing to enter the monastery. The Elder received me kindly and asked who I was and where I was from. Having listened to me he replied: 'The Lord Himself will show you your path.' I wanted then to stay in Shcheglov, but the Elder again told me: 'Your path is a different one. The Lord Himself will show you.' In the same year, July 17, 1906, I entered the Hermitage of St. Tikhon in Kaluga province."[1]

2. THE MONASTERY OF ST. TIKHON

This beautifully situated monastery was founded in the 15th century by a hermit, St. Tikhon, who lived first in the renowned Chudov monastery in Moscow, but did not stay there long. Yearning for the solitary life, or perhaps being judged ready for it with his abba's blessing, St. Tikhon left the noisy capital and went deep into the wild country of the Kaluga region, then covered with dense, impenetrable forests. There he later founded a monastery dedicated to the Dormition of the Mother of God, which flourished in the 16th century and was destroyed in 1610 during the Time of Troubles.

About this monastery Fr. Gerasim wrote: "Not long before the revolution, St. Tikhon's Monastery, which had retained the title of a desert hermitage, 'blossomed like a lily' and was one of the best established of all desert monasteries. About two miles from the monastery was the spring of St. Tikhon with two separate, enclosed pools built into the healing well; a church; and two houses where the monastic brotherhood, consisting of seven or eight monks,

---

1. From the periodical *Orthodox Carpathian Russia*, 1934.

lived at that time. Eight miles from the monastery was a skete dedicated to the Meeting of the Lord, inhabited by thirty monks. In the skete the humble and quiet brotherhood spent its time in hard ascetic labors. The skete was located deep in the forest, and only later did the sound of the railroad tracks, which were constructed nearby, disrupt the quietness of this wondrous spot in one of the most picturesque areas of the Kaluga region."[2]

In the 1830's the monks and elders of Optina Monastery took pains to restore the spiritual life in St. Tikhon's Monastery. Elder Moses put special love into this holy work and many times used to send Elder Leonid with his disciples there. Elder Anthony sent there his spiritual son, Schema-monk Sergius[3] (Simeon Yanovsky), who had originally been converted by St. Herman of Alaska. The monastery of St. Tikhon was not far from Optina. Between these two monasteries there was constant contact. Fr. Gerasim recalled: "Optina and its elders were well known to me from childhood."

3. A MIRACLE OF ST. TIKHON

Before coming to St. Tikhon's Monastery to stay, Fr. Gerasim received miraculous help from the monastery's patron himself. "In my youth," he wrote, "I fell into a river early in the spring and caught a bad cold. I had frightful pains in the joints of my legs. In the morning I would be unable to unbend my joints, the pain was frightful, and I would cry.

"One splendid summer we went on foot to the monastery of St. Tikhon of Kaluga, which was about fifty miles from our city. I can tell you that for me this was a great labor. At times I could hardly walk; the pain in my knees tormented me.

"In St. Tikhon's Monastery there is the healing well of St. Tikhon a mile or more from the monastery. The water is fresh, clear as crystal, and frightfully cold.

---

2. From the periodical *Pravoslavny Blagovestnik*, San Francisco, January, 1943.

3. Fr. Gerasim spoke of how he used to care for the grave of Fr. Sergius.

FR. GERASIM'S FRIENDS AT THE CHOIR PRACTICE OF ST. TIKHON'S
MONASTERY, 1906.

On the back of this photograph Fr. Gerasim has written: "1) Choir-master Gury, in schema Fr. Gideon [standing, at center], died on Mount Athos 45 years ago in St. Andrew's Skete. 2) Novice John, who kneels in the picture [the second kneeling person from left], left St. Tikhon's Monastery in August, 1906, and lived on Mount Athos. In monasticism he was Barsanuphius, in schema Basil. He reposed during the World War in his hermitage. 3) The Elder with the book [standing, at far left] is Hieromonk Tikhon, sacristan, who died in September, 1906. And only God knows what happened to the others.
A. Gerasim"

"Going there, I undressed myself, prayed, and began to immerse myself in the water. At first a powerful pain burned me, but I still went into the water and immersed myself three times over my head, and then went out to where all the pilgrims were dressing. An unearthly joy took possession of me, of my soul, and I became joyful and happy. The pain had vanished. Returning home, I walked rapidly and even carried my mother's and aunt's purses. And afterwards for many years I had no pain in my legs."[4]

4. ELDER IOASAPH

Upon entering St. Tikhon's Monastery as a novice, Fr. Gerasim was entrusted to the holy Elder Ioasaph and given an obedience in the infirmary. There he received a sound monastic formation; and his understanding of monasticism remained to the end of his life genuine, firm and sober. "God granted me to live in St. Tikhon's Monastery for about six years," he wrote, "becoming well-acquainted with the entire expanse of the monastery. Before the First World War there were 250 brothers in the monastery."[5]

About his elder, Fr. Gerasim wrote: "In the monastery of St. Tikhon I had a most kind elder, Fr. Ioasaph, in the world John Nekrasov. He brilliantly finished the course of the Tula seminary; he was the son of a priest and a relative of Metropolitan Isidore. After finishing the course he began working at the Holy Synod. But he was inclined to monastery life and visited Old Valaam. He could not stay there, however, as the damp climate was bad for him and he suffered with fever. He returned to St. Petersburg, resigned his post, and went to Moscow to seek a monastery.

"He entered the St. Nicholas of Ugresh Monastery and stayed there for three years. The brothers in our Russian monasteries were mostly peasants, and most of the superiors were also. Some of them were crude, lovers of authority, and did not like educated people. And it was because of the crudeness of the Archimandrite that Brother John Nekrasov left this monastery and hastened to Optina

---

4. "The Life of St. Tikhon of Kaluga," in *The Orthodox Word*, no. 91, p. 78.
5. *Pravoslavny Blagovestnik*, January, 1943.

Monastery, which at this time was renowned throughout Russia for its elders.

"Brother John came to Optina and went to Elder Macarius for counsel. Fr. Macarius listened to him and then told him: 'Go, Brother John, to St. Tikhon's Monastery, and finish your earthly life there.' And so he went there and was tonsured with the name Ioasaph, and lived there more than fifty years."[6]

Fr. Gerasim's monastic training under the guidance of elders and preceptors who were the offspring of the great Optina Monastery formed his soul and prepared him for his diligent service to God and man. Many years later he was to write of Optina and Kaluga: "These are my native places, precious ones. The days of my youth, the golden years of my monastic life were spent there. . . . For a monk it is sweeter to be with God in the desert, farther away from the world, from its temptations."

5. TWO ELDER GERASIMS

In the St. Tikhon of Kaluga Monastery there lived another ascetic who had been sent from Optina, Elder Gerasim (†1898), a disciple of Optina Elder Ambrose. Having come to St. Tikhon's Monastery eight years after the death of this Elder Gerasim, our Fr. Gerasim heard much about his holy life and recorded for posterity a miraculous incident related to him. This Elder, he wrote, "conceived the idea of building a women's convent about eight miles from St. Tikhon's Monastery. Good people had already given him the land; it was a very beautiful place and suitable for a monastery. Elder Gerasim made a petition to the Holy Synod asking permission for him to begin building a monastery in honor of the Iveron Mother of God. For a long time there was no answer from the Synod, and the Elder already began to think that his good intention was not to be realized.

"One beautiful spring day he went to the place where he intended to build a monastery. He prayed fervently at the forest

---

6. Archimandrite Gerasim, "The New Martyrs of Kaluga," in *The Orthodox Word*, no. 91, p. 75.

meadow and after prayer lay down on the green grass and fell asleep. In a dream he saw a tall monk in the schema, with a noble appearance, come up to him and say: 'Do not grieve, Father, but hurry to the monastery; they are waiting for you there — the papers have come from the Synod.'

" 'And who are you, Father?!' Elder Gerasim asked the monk.

" 'I am the disciple of St. Tikhon, Schema-monk Philaret, and my grave is there.' He pointed to his grave.

"Elder Gerasim woke up, gave thanks to the Lord for His wondrous and consoling dream, and prayed fervently, at the place indicated by the monk, for the repose of Schema-monk Philaret. He hastened to the monastery, and what did he find? They were waiting for him; a package had arrived from the Synod, and a blessing had been given for the building of a holy monastery."

"I myself," Fr. Gerasim continues, ". . . prayed at the grave of Schema-monk Philaret. Elder Gerasim built a chapel over it and an ever-burning icon lamp illuminated it. Up to then no one had known that a disciple of St. Tikhon was lying there. . . .

"Elder Gerasim soon built there a splendid women's convent (where Abbess Sophia, the later new martyr, placed the beginning of her monastic life)."

Fr. Gerasim, then the novice Michael, visited this convent in April of 1914. Sitting on the balcony of the guesthouse, he was awed by the magnificent setting: the convent, which had been built on a bluff above the river Oka, was filled with lilac bushes and birch trees. The monastery cemetery was aglow with the light of a multitude of memorial lamps. It was a sight he could never forget.

Although Fr. Gerasim never personally met the first Elder Gerasim of the Kaluga monastery, he did know the Elder's disciple, who received the same name and came to be known as Elder Gerasim the Younger (†1918). Like Fr. Gerasim, Elder Gerasim the Younger was known as Michael (Misha) before his monastic tonsure. He became as clairvoyant as his Elder, who once told him, "Misha, you will become higher than me." He founded the St. Sergius Skete, where he gave spiritual healing to many suffering ones. He and

General view of St. Tikhon's Monastery, 1907.

Elder Gerasim of St. Tikhon's Monastery

Elder Gerasim the Younger

Abbess Sophia were close friends and would send visitors to one another for help and consolation. Grand-Duchess Elizabeth Feodorovna, after the death of Elder Gabriel of Pskov, went to this Elder Gerasim the Younger for spiritual direction.

6. MOUNT ATHOS

In 1911 Fr. Gerasim, still a novice, fulfilled his childhood dream and went to the monastic kingdom of Mount Athos, Greece. "I decided to remain there forever," he wrote, "and entered the novitiate in the Brotherhood of St. Andrew's Russian Skete." Soon, however, his father died, and he felt he should return to Russia to console his ailing mother. He was torn between this duty and his desire to stay on the Holy Mountain, when a certain occurrence finally decided the question for him. "Once I saw in my dream," he recalled, "Monk Christopher from my St. Tikhon's Monastery, who had died on the 11th of January, 1911. I saw him walking on a green meadow. The sun was brightly shining all over. Having caught up with me, Fr. Christopher said to me, 'Greetings, Father.' And then he added, 'You should leave this place, and as soon as possible.' I asked him, 'Where do you live now, Fr. Christopher?' 'Same place — there in St. Tikhon's Monastery,' he answered. Then we turned east, and I saw as if the whole of St. Tikhon's Monastery was placed on a green meadow bathed in sunlight. It was such a beauty: all was blindingly white; the crosses, as if pure gold, were brightly burning on the majestic cathedral and belfry. Then Fr. Christopher led me to the Transfiguration Catholicon, where the relics of St. Tikhon were treasured under the reliquary eaves. I was amazed at its beauty and the luxury of its decoration. Fr. Christopher was a great ascetic. His main virtues were that he never judged anyone and never visited anyone, knowing only the temple of God and his humble cell. I woke up and began to think of what I had seen in my dream.

"I had known Fr. Christopher very well; he used to love me. Involuntarily I began to wonder about the dream I had seen and decided to leave not only Mount Athos but even the Athonite Metochion in Odessa, to which I had been appointed to do my obedience. My monk-friends called me to go to Tula, to the Protection of the Mother of God city monastery, where there was a dire need for working monks. In 1912, right on the Feast of the Protection of the Mother of God, I arrived in Tula and began to live a quiet life working in the temple."[7]

7. ELDER IOASAPH'S PROPHECY

Fr. Gerasim's elder at St. Tikhon's Monastery, Fr. Ioasaph, had already hinted to him what course his life would take. As Fr. Gerasim recalled, "Fr. Ioasaph was a doer of the mental Jesus Prayer, and he was a clairvoyant elder. Two years before I left St. Tikhon's Monastery he told me, 'Misha, a learned hierarch will meet you, will take a liking to you, and soon you will receive everything like a learned man.' Such words he repeated several times.

"But at that time could I, the poor novice Michael, even think that a learned bishop would come to like me? Indeed, I was afraid of bishops; my hands trembled as I held the service book when I served in the altar for a bishop. But still everything Elder Ioasaph told me came to pass.

"In 1912 I returned from Athos and stayed in Tula, where the monastic metochion of Bishop Evdokim was located. There were only a few brothers there; no one wished to live in a poor, unorganized monastery. I stayed, and Vladika[8] gave me my favorite obedience — that of sacristan. True, there was a lot of work. The church was immense. I loved icon lamps and adorned the whole church with them. I lived there in peace and quiet. The people in Tula were good, believing people. Vladika Evdokim liked me and entrusted the whole church and sacristy to me. Our services were solemn. In 1914 four altars were consecrated and the cathedral was beautiful.

"Vladika often visited my cell and conversed with me for hours. We talked of building a bell-tower and cells for the brothers.

---

7. From the Harbin (Manchuria) Church periodical *Khleb Nebesny (Heavenly Bread)*, no. 11, pp. 14-17.

8. *Vladika:* an endearing term for a bishop.

But unexpectedly, on June 30, 1914, Vladika was assigned to North America. And so the words of Elder Ioasaph were fulfilled."

In these recollections we see how Fr. Gerasim's life's path was led by grace, and how one event was organically linked to another to serve God's designs. His soul was open to God's every call, and he answered it time and again.[9]

8. ARRIVAL IN AMERICA

Bishop Evdokim, although he met an unfortunate end, vividly embodied the highest aspirations and the energetic direction of the most progressive leaders and minds of the Russian Orthodox Church. Meeting him, the young novice Michael was filled with his missionary fervor and chose to temporarily accompany him to North America. They arrived in New York City on May 4th, 1915. At first assisting the Bishop, he was soon tonsured and given the name Gerasim in honor of the two great luminaries of Kaluga. In time he was destined to become the *third* righteous Gerasim from St. Tikhon's Monastery.

That same year, being only 27 years old, he was ordained deacon and then priest, and served in Chicago. His first trial as a priest occurred soon after his ordination; and his reaction to it was very indicative of his character. It was the Sunday during Great Lent when the Church commemorates the Last Judgement. A certain Bishop, having ordained Fr. Gerasim just months before, told him to go to the ambo and give a sermon. "Go out there and scare them up a bit," the Bishop said. *"There won't be a Last Judgment anyway,* but the people need a little shaking up." Fr. Gerasim stood there dumbfounded, hardly able to believe his ears. It was as if, he said later, someone had just dumped a bucket of ice water over him. There before him was the Bishop who had given him apostolic succession, had made him a priest by the laying on of hands; and that Bishop was just treating the Church like a form, with no content. Seeing Fr. Gerasim's speechlessness and incredulous ex-

---

9. *The Orthodox Word,* no. 91, pp. 75-76.

Fr. Gerasim after his ordination as a hieromonk, 1915.

pression, he slapped him on the back. "What's the matter?" he asked. "Don't be a wet hen. Go out there and give it to them!"

And Fr. Gerasim did just that. Stepping out of the altar, he saw before him the guileless faces of loving people who *did* believe, just like himself. He knew what he had to say. As the Bishop listened on, Fr. Gerasim spoke out boldly and with conviction against the sin of unbelief, against mere formalism and ritualism in church life. "If we go to church and do all the outward things to be seen by others, without truly believing in our hearts, this is HYPOCRISY!" he exclaimed. "Nothing is hidden from God. At the LAST JUDGMENT, He will judge what is in our hearts and convict us of our unbelief." By the end of his sermon, many of the believers were moved to tears at the power of his words.

To his disappointment, Fr. Gerasim found that other clergy with whom he came into contact were also spiritually bankrupt, viewing their missionary work as part of an existing cultural establishment. Seizing the opportunity anew he answered the missionary call and travelled to Alaska with Bishop Philip in 1916. He went first to Sitka, then to Kodiak, and finally was assigned as a village priest on the island of Afognak, where he spent eighteen years.

9. THE CRUCIFIXION OF HOLY RUSSIA

When the Revolution of 1917 broke out in Russia, Fr. Gerasim saw a dream: "The whole sky was dark, fearful. But in the midst of it there was light, and there was Christ crucified. He was dying; His head was bent down and the muscles on His arms trembled from suffering. And I heard a voice: 'Pray; Russia is crucified.' And soon we in Alaska heard of the fierce persecution of Christian believers and the destruction of holy places. His Elder Ioasaph met such a fate. "He died on January 2, 1919," Fr. Gerasim related, "on the feast of St. Seraphim, after the brothers had already been banished from the monastery. And as the last abbot of the monastery, Fr. Jonah, wrote me, he died of starvation." From Kaluga Fr. Gerasim received letters from Fr. Job the iconographer, who told him of the martyred Elder Zosima, an ascetic who lived in a cabin in the forest beyond

Hieromonk Gerasim in 1916,
the year he arrived in Alaska.

THE CHURCH OF THE NATIVITY OF THE THEOTOKOS
on the island of Afognak, where Fr. Gerasim served for 18 years.
At left is the house he lived in.

the monastery. Fr. Job wrote: "We have had new martyrs among us after the overthrow of the Tsar. Some hooligans tied up Elder Zosima and burned his forest cabin. His burned bones were brought to the monastery. Our brothers were all the time working on the farm doing the work themselves. In the autumn they began to bring to the monastery whatever was gathered during the summer, and some young hoodlums attacked and beat them up terribly. Some of them were crippled for life. They did inhuman things to the defenseless monks, tearing out the hair on their heads and beards. . . . And many have already departed into another world." The Bolsheviks soon banished Fr. Job to Siberia. Twelve years later he returned to find the St. Tikhon of Kaluga Monastery devoid of monks and desecrated by the atheists. He was soon caught and sent again to Siberia, from where Fr. Gerasim received the last letter from him.

With lamentation Fr. Gerasim bore in his heart this great burden for his native land and friends. In later years he wrote: "One becomes so sad when one remembers Russia, the Bolshevik Russia, where the red dragon has been installed and tortures both the body and soul of the Russian people. Oh Lord, save it! . . . I love my land, and I shed tears over it in my solitude." And again: "1918 arrived and the beautiful monastery of St. Tikhon was taken over and defiled by the godless ones. The monks were forced to leave, the holy things were desecrated, the bells and crosses, taken down. It is difficult for me even to remember that. My tears do not allow me to write."[10]

10. THE CALL OF ST. HERMAN

Spruce Island, Alaska, located between the Kodiak and Afognak islands, had in the last century been the home of the holy monk and missionary, St. Herman (†1836). Having come to America from the Valaam island monastery in Russia, he had named Spruce Island "New Valaam."

---

10. *Pravoslavny Blagovestnik*, 1943.

Fr. Gerasim first visited Spruce Island on May 27, 1927, soon after the radiant Feast of Easter. It was a quiet, sunny morning. He was accompanied by Archpriest Nicholas Kashevarov and two female pilgrims. On the site of the hut where St. Herman had lived, and which had now completely disintegrated, there stood only a wooden memorial. A little further on there was a church over the grave of the blessed Elder, and there Fr. Gerasim served a panikhida.[11] It was a glorious day; spring birds were singing; and Fr. Gerasim liked the spot very much. It didn't seem like Alaska, but rather like some monastery in Russia. On the way back they again came to the clearing in the woods where St. Herman had lived and where on his deathbed he had shone with the light of Mt. Tabor, his cell being filled with the fragrance of heavenly incense. While his companions went on ahead, Fr. Gerasim kneeled down and, overwhelmed with joy, exclaimed: "Christ is risen, Fr. Herman!" Suddenly he sensed in the air a marvelous fragrance of incense surrounding him. He even shuddered. He thought that it might have come from the cassock of Fr. Nicholas, but the latter was dressed in an overcoat and was already too far away. And the aroma was such a fine one, and so pleasant! With a quiet joy in his heart he then addressed the Elder as if he were alive: "I thank you, dear Elder, Fr. Herman, that you have found me worthy to visit this beloved spot of yours! Fr. Herman, I too have fallen dearly in love with this spot; if there should come a time when I will be able to come here to you to stay — accept me!"

Of extraordinary interest is this prophecy of St. Herman. Bishop Peter of New Archangel (Sitka), reported in 1867 the following prediction: "Still more he (Fr. Herman) used to say that although a long time would pass after his death, he would not be forgotten, and the place where he used to live would not be deserted; that a monk like himself, fleeing worldly glory, would come and live on Spruce Island."[12]

---

11. *Panikhida:* a service for the dead.
12. *Outline of the History of the American Orthodox Mission* (in Russian), Valaam Monastery, St. Petersburg, 1894, p. 179.

In 1927, soon after this visit to Spruce Island, Fr. Gerasim would write: "It is a great pity that there is no one there. There were two families who settled there, but they started to make beer and carouse. The Elder quickly drove them away. . . . Now the Elder again abides there in solitude."

11. EARTHLY HINDRANCES

About the same time Fr. Gerasim was joined for a while in Afognak by the future Athonite hermit, Father Nikon, and together they shared their monastic dreams and expectations, recalling bright, joyous memories of Holy Russia. Fr. Nikon, however, soon left for Mount Athos and settled in the cell of St. George in Karoulia. It was this Fr. Nikon who persuaded the now famous E. Kadloubovsky and G. E. H. Palmer to translate the *Philokalia* for the first time into English.

Having beheld the cataclysmic crucifixion of Holy Russia and the desolation of the holy places, which persists to the present day, Fr. Gerasim treasured dearly that rich monastic tradition in which he had providentially immersed himself and which he had known in full bloom. In 1926, when Russian bishops in America broke away from other, more traditional and monastically-minded Russian bishops in the free world, Fr. Gerasim's conscience could not go along with this, even though all of Orthodox Alaska blindly followed the schism. Fr. Gerasim remained alone, isolated, not only outwardly, but without anyone of like mind for thousands of miles. In the late 1920's, due to the intolerable attitude of the surrounding clergy he even left Alaska for a while to serve in Washington State and in British Columbia; but true to his divine call he returned for good to stand at his post as an outcast. His stand caused great displeasure on the part of the local clergy. He turned to St. Herman for help. Within nine years he had made the final decision to leave his parish altogether and seek refuge on Fr. Herman's island.

In 1935, at the end of August, when it became known that Fr. Gerasim was preparing to go to the island to live, the local clergy opposed this and resolved to prevent it. Vassily Skvortsov, who had intended to accompany Fr. Gerasim, came to him in Afognak and informed him that they were going to expel him from the hermitage with the aid of the police. He himself, out of fear, had decided not to go. Fr. Gerasim was very much affected by this, but he replied that if it wasn't going to be pleasing to Fr. Herman, then that's how it was going to be. He was so disturbed about it that before going to bed he hadn't even strength enough to say his prayers.

Then he had a dream, in which he was walking somewhere through a beautiful forest: spruce trees, in the distance a hill, and straight ahead a clearing with tall grass. And he heard someone pealing a bell and its sound joyfully echoing somewhere nearby. In the clearing he saw two bushy little spruce trees, and between them a monk of small stature with a thin little beard and wearing a small monk's cap. He smiled and greeted Fr. Gerasim, saying: "It is I who am here ringing the Easter bells." And then kindly: "Batiushka,[13] don't be sad! It is Fr. S---y who stirs people against you. Have patience and all will pass! . . . " At this the dream ended. In the morning Fr. Gerasim got up joyfully and resolved that there was no one to fear if St. Herman was with him.

12. THE BUILDING OF A SKETE

On September 8, 1935, Fr. Gerasim abandoned everything, and taking his abbot's staff went to guard the Saint's premises, becoming the one guiding light of 20th-century Orthodox Alaska. The Saint, looking down from above, blessed this fearless witnessing of the truth and made his prophecy be fulfilled upon Fr. Gerasim, who bore the same name as St. Herman's beloved disciple.[14]

Fr. Gerasim lived on the island for the next thirty years, alone among the age-old spruce trees and gloomy storms. Since no one besides him had lived so long on the island's holy site at Monks'

---

13. *Batiushka:* "little father" — the affectionate name by which Russians address their priests.

14. This disciple was a young Creole man who spent much time with St. Herman and later recounted his miracles. There is also strong historical evidence to suggest that St. Herman's name before becoming a monk was Gerasim.

Fr. Gerasim in front of his Spruce Island cell, Pascha, 1936.

St. Herman ringing the Paschal bells, as he appeared to Fr. Gerasim.
Iconographic painting by Gleb Podmoshensky, 1961.

THE CHAPEL OF THE KALUGA MOTHER OF GOD
which Fr. Gerasim built on Spruce Island over the site of St. Herman's cell.

THE INTERIOR OF THE CHAPEL
with a large Kaluga Icon of the Mother of God above the altar.

Fr. Gerasim in front of the Kaluga Mother of God chapel, 1961.

Belongings of St. Herman which Fr. Gerasim treasured in the Kaluga Mother of God chapel, on the site of St. Herman's deathbed. Included are St. Herman's klobuk (monastic hat), his chains, and his cross.

Lagoon since the death of St. Herman, he was undoubtedly the very monk "fleeing worldly glory," about whom the Wonderworker of Alaska had prophesied more than a hundred years before.

During the spring following his arrival on Spruce Island, Fr. Gerasim wrote: "I decided to abandon Afognak, where I lived for 19 years. And tears again...."

He first wanted to build a chapel behind Monks' Lagoon, on the spot where St. Herman had once built his half-earthen cell and where he had died. Not having any support from church authorities, he financed the building himself with money he had earned by creating beautiful works of embroidery — a talent he had learned from his dear mother. As the chapel was being built with the help of some Aleut natives, he described it thus: "Its size is 14 x 12 feet. It is wooden and the inside is covered by plywood. It has two windows. Everything should be simple there, just as was the humble cell of Fr. Herman. But I will turn it into the Greek "Paraklis"; that is, a small chapel without an iconostasis, only a curtain. I will see what can be done. But I am limitlessly happy that my wish has come true, that a chapel has already been erected on the spot where for a whole 40 years a bright candle burned, where lived a great righteous man who prayed for the sinful world — Fr. Herman. I want so much to resurrect that which is dear and akin to me, that which is holy, here in this land, when in my native land everything is destroyed. One wishes so much to see this dear skete, a skete that would be filled with prayer near the grave of the holy elder. A skete . . . O Lord, help!"

The chapel, dedicated to the Kaluga Icon of the Mother of God, had above the altar a large copy of this icon. The warmth and tenderness of the icon, and in fact of the whole chapel, evoked contrition of heart in those who visited it, and called to mind the blessed realm of Russian piety in which Fr. Gerasim still abided, so far from his homeland.

Fr. Gerasim settled in a small, cozy cabin which he built next to this chapel. Reflecting on his move he later wrote: "If I hadn't moved to Spruce Island in 1935, there would be nothing but ruins there now." A white church dedicated to Sts. Sergius and Herman of

THE CHURCH OF STS. SERGIUS AND HERMAN OF VALAAM
as it looked when Fr. Gerasim arrived on Spruce Island.
From the collection of M. Z. Vinokouroff, Alaska Historical Library.

THE SAME CHURCH AFTER FR. GERASIM RESTORED IT
Underneath is the grave of St. Herman. Fr. Gerasim kept the
Saint's relics inside the church itself.

THE INTERIOR OF THE STS. SERGIUS AND HERMAN CHURCH

At right is the reliquary of St. Herman. In the corner is an icon of the Mother of God as the Abbess of Mount Athos, and thus the protector and guide of all monastics.

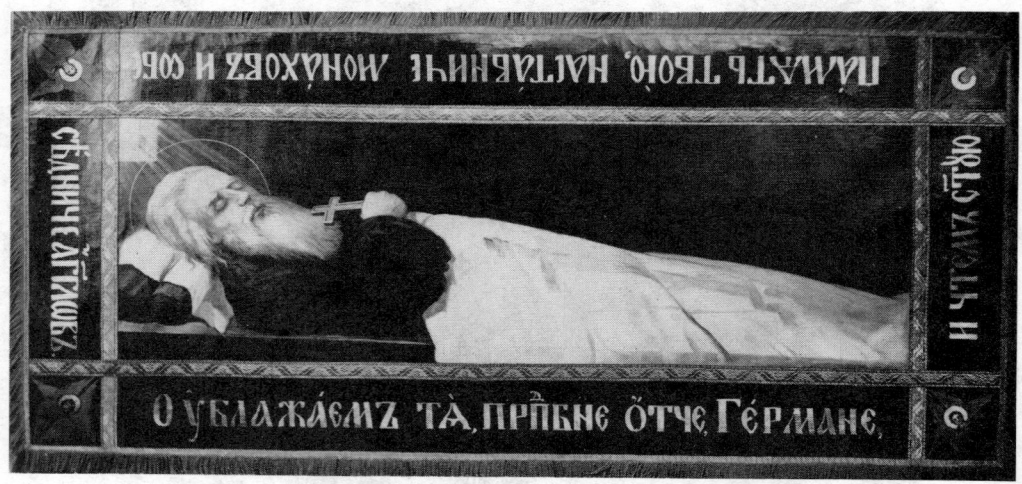

THE COVERING OF ST. HERMAN'S RELIQUARY

painted by Archimandrite Seraphim Oblivantseff at the request of Fr. Gerasim. The Slavonic writing around it reads: "We glorify thee, holy Father Herman, and we honor thy holy memory, instructor of monks and converser with angels."

Valaam had been built over St. Herman's grave at the turn of the century; but due to time and the severely damp climate it had almost decayed by the time Fr. Gerasim moved there. In the late 1930's he completely restored it. When the foundation was being laid, the coffin with the remains of St. Herman was damaged, and the relics were transferred into a new coffin and placed in the chapel at the right side of the entrance.

13. MICHAEL Z. VINOKOUROFF

Michael Z. Vinokouroff, an archivist of Russian-American manuscripts for the Library of Congress, had in the course of his research developed a great love for St. Herman. Having heard rumors that Fr. Gerasim had done "unlawful things" with the relics of St. Herman, he went to Alaska in 1940 to "save St. Herman" from the clutches of "a fanatic hermit." Utilizing a commission to go and save church records from abandoned chapels in Alaska, he came to Spruce Island with, as he said, "hatred in his heart" — only to meet a man who genuinely loved St. Herman and who lived in poverty, enduring cold and loneliness for the sake of keeping alive the "monastic lamp" that had been lit by St. Herman on "New Valaam." The quick mind of Vinokouroff immediately sized up the situation, and his wrath turned into love. His subsequent lifelong friendship with Fr. Gerasim resulted in several hundreds of pages of priceless correspondence, which reveal the inner life of the desert-dweller of Spruce Island. Vinokouroff's appreciation of the truthful stand of St. Herman was the basis of his both discovering and valuing Fr. Gerasim so much. He helped Fr. Gerasim to go on by encouraging him in his adamant stand and faithful Orthodox witness. In so doing, he at the same time enabled the young generation of today to receive a healthy patristic transmission through one of the rare carriers of the spirit of Holy Russia.

A very striking personality, Vinokouroff was a brilliant man in his own right. His judgement of Fr. Gerasim, which was formed by his warm heart as well as by his ability to soberly and precisely appraise things of historic value, is indicative of Fr. Gerasim's true

ARCHIMANDRITE GERASIM
(1888-1969)
This photograph is from a Christmas card that Fr. Gerasim sent to his friend Vinokouroff.

MICHAEL Z. VINOKOUROFF
(1894-1983)

significance. He once said that Fr. Gerasim was "on the right post" — at a time when no one else except the simple Aleuts shared this opinion.

It is interesting that Fr. Gerasim died on Vinokouroff's nameday (in 1969), and Vinokouroff died on Fr. Gerasim's nameday in the world (in 1983). Thus, even in death they were united.

14. A SOLITARY STAND

In the 1930's there were unsuccessful attempts to build a monastery on Spruce Island by bishops who knew nothing of monasticism; one of them had never even heard of St. Seraphim of Sarov until Fr. Gerasim told him of this Saint, for whom he had a particular devotion. They even tried to drive Fr. Gerasim off the island; and the natives of Kodiak then collected 250 signatures on a petition to allow him to stay. The local church authorities sent other monks to live on Spruce Island, intending to create an uncharitable rivalry that would squeeze Fr. Gerasim right off the island or at least make him miserable. Though some of the monks who tried to settle there had honest intentions and genuine monastic interests, they were just the tools of those who sought a merely political hegemony in their locality. Not having been called to live at New Valaam by St. Herman himself, as had Fr. Gerasim, these monks eventually left.

The most audacious attempt to drive Fr. Gerasim off the island occurred during World War II, when rumors were circulated and even published that Fr. Gerasim was actually Gregory Rasputin and had gone to Spruce Island to "hide out"! The military, which had a naval look-out on the island at the time, were told to investigate, and came to search through Fr. Gerasim's papers and belongings. Thus Fr. Gerasim was put in the ridiculous position of having to "prove" he wasn't Rasputin, who had been dead for over twenty years!

Fr. Gerasim could have laid a firm foundation for a monastery on Spruce Island had it not been for the destructive ecclesiastical climate, which made him suffer for his refusal to be partisan in church politics. When asked, "Which jurisdiction do you belong to?" he would reply to all: "To Christ's jurisdiction!" "Yes, according to

Fr. Gerasim (holding staff) with the work crew of Bishop Alexey, who in the 1930's made an abortive attempt at establishing a monastery on Spruce Island.

The house that Bishop Alexey had built on Icon Bay, adjacent to Monks' Lagoon. When the Bishop's plans failed, the native Aleuts moved this house to the shore of Monks' Lagoon, where it stands to this day.

Christ's commandment," he wrote, "I pray for all, I commemorate all," no matter what administrative "jurisdiction" they belonged to. But the separation between the Russian churches in the free world, he added, "hurts me very much."

Although unsuccessful in establishing an organized monastery, Fr. Gerasim potentially fulfilled St. Herman's wish for a monastery on the island. By his settling at Monks' Lagoon in the desert tradition of St. Herman, there were united in him, despite all his shortcomings, the highest monastic strivings of his dear Mount Athos, from where he received periodic reports that the Russian monks were rapidly dying out, of his native Optina and Kaluga Monasteries; and of St. Herman's beloved Valaam. Through him, the men of prayer of these quintessential shrines of Orthodox piety march across time and space, join us, and taking us by the hand demonstrate the realistic possibility of the union of God and man which lies at the very heart of the monastic life. Fr. Gerasim truly kept vigil over this cumulative patristic experience, this love of beauty, this sweet melancholic longing, a longing to retain, embrace and drink the holiness which earlier he had encountered so often, in so many places; this holiness which had been indelibly deposited by St. Herman on these very shores, on the very spot where he now stood. In the golden years of his monastic life he had learned this fidelity to the desert ideal, whose beauty he continually extolled as the criterion by which he lived his solitary life on New Valaam. In 1959, reflecting upon his life of solitude, he wrote, "All these 23 years in my beloved, quiet desert have been dear to me. Every time I pray before the grave of Elder Herman, I thank him that he accepted me, that he took me into his monastery, into his quiet desert. Last summer I served 45 Liturgies there. But now because of ill health I've been detained here and I miss my desert."

15. SPIRITUAL TEACHING

In his last years, the ailing Fr. Gerasim was forced to spend winters in the Aleut village of Ouzinkie, on the opposite side of the island. There he would perform services in the village church and

Fr. Gerasim leading a procession in front of the Kodiak church of the Resurrection.

provide spiritual guidance for the people. To this day, the villagers remember him with tremendous love, as the only pastor since St. Herman who was a true father to them. He did not hesitate to both console and rebuke his children in order to keep them on the right path. Since drunkenness was a problem among the villagers, he was outspoken in his condemnation of this sin.

Being a warm-hearted, down-to-earth person, Fr. Gerasim was not at all hard to get to know. When he would visit people in Ouzinkie or when they would come to him at Monks' Lagoon — often bringing mail, freshly-caught fish, and a share of their provisions — he would fill them with wonderful stories from his own Holy Russia. His endearing tales would alternately bring them to contrite tears and innocent laughter, evoking in them compassion, cheerfulness and good will towards God's creatures and the whole world.

He especially loved to tell of the Lives of Saints. Here he was in his own element, amidst the world of angelic men and women who inspired him to persevere along his most arduous path. He had precisely the right "feel" for the saints; and this, combined with his remarkable teaching gift, enabled him to convey their true spirit with an effectiveness that is all but unheard of nowadays. Fortunate were those children who heard of the saints from his lips. His godson Gene Sundberg, who grew up to be his devoted friend, recalls how, as a child, he would be enthralled by Fr. Gerasim's stories. Seeing the avidness of his little listener, Fr. Gerasim would become all inspired himself and go on and on about the saints. "I wanted him never to stop"; Gene remembers, "and I would dread the time when my mother would inevitably come in and say it was time for bed."

16. LAST YEARS

Fr. Gerasim was in many ways like a free-spirited and joyful child. His visitors and spiritual children remember how, while performing daily duties at his desert hermitage, he could not help but break into song, remembering folk melodies from his happy childhood. But beneath this was the tribulation that is the lot of all true monks, and indeed of all true servants of God in this world. "Yes," he wrote, "I had to suffer here persecution, slander and insults, but not from Communists, not from American unbelievers, no, but from 'humble' bishops and my own brethren. And here I have been working in Alaska for 49 years. And all these years have been lived by me in strict poverty, in cold. And for all these long years I did not have a warm nook. But, of course, I know what our great martyr, the Russian people, is suffering, and I pray for it and suffer all. Indeed, I did not seek in America either a good parish or a warmer climate. I love my little hermitage and I wish to lay down my bones here. Yea, may it be so! May it be so!"[15]

And the Lord granted Fr. Gerasim to find his final resting place on Spruce Island, even though for the last several years of his life, to his great sorrow, he was unable to live there. After the disastrous earthquake and tidal wave of March 27, 1964, in which he almost lost his life, being in the flood waters up to his neck, Fr. Gerasim's health declined; and in September, 1965, Gene Sundberg (who supplied the information that follows in quotes) brought him to Kodiak and took care of him.

In the last year Fr. Gerasim "became so forgetful that the only thought left in his mind was to get to Monks' Lagoon and Fr. Herman. . . . He then started wandering at night." Since June of 1969 he was in a Kodiak hospital, where in October he developed double pneumonia. On Sunday, October 12, he received Holy Communion and in the evening Holy Unction. "Fr. Gerasim requested it and hung on till the last prayer, and when it was finished, just peacefully left us. . . . It was so beautiful, I know I smiled. . . . There was no pain, no strain, no effort."

After the funeral service on October 15, "the sea was rough, but the best captains felt we could make it. . . . After a fairly rough trip we landed at Pestrikoff beach and began the most exhilarating experience I have ever had. . . . About a hundred men, women and children made the trek. After a two-hour walk we arrived at the spot he picked for himself 32 years ago, and there he was laid to rest in the place he loved best and near the one he loved best, his

---

15. From a letter to the Russian periodical *Free Word*, 1965, nos. 73-74.

Above: funeral procession of Fr. Gerasim on Spruce Island, led by Bishop Theodosius of Sitka. The cross is the one planted by Fr. Gerasim 32 years before on the site of his own grave.

At right: Fr. Gerasim's grave at Monks' Lagoon, as it looks today.

Fr. Herman. Some people said the birds began to sing as if welcoming him back home. Others said there were sweet fragrances, and some even said they felt as though Fr. Herman was watching us. . . . His burial was somewhat comparable to Fr. Herman's, in that there weren't enough priests to bury him and so the natives whom he taught and loved carried him to his resting place. The sea was stormy too, but not enough to keep us away."[16]

17. HIS SIGNIFICANCE

In the ranks of Orthodox righteous ones of the 20th century, Fr. Gerasim was above all a *confessor*. He was entrusted with a "little thing": the guarding of a saint's relics. But as Christ said: "He that is faithful in that which is least is faithful also in much" (Luke 16:10). And Fr. Gerasim was truly faithful: against all obstacles he remained unwavering on this post. Although abandoned and outwardly defenseless, he with God's help stood in firm defense of the traditional, *ascetic* way of seeing reality, which so few around him understood. In his righteous death this suffering old man became a hero for the future — an inspiration for young idealists of new generations, and a shining example of steadfastness and constancy in an age of relativism, lukewarmness and betrayal. Even today there are young monastics who, drawing strength from his heroic witness, are living on his New Valaam, keeping alive the "monastic lamp" that he lit anew on the island.

May we never forget him, and may his life encourage us to also remain, no matter what tribulations may come, at the "post" which God has for each and every one of us. †

The Monks of New Valaam
The 20th Anniversary of Fr. Gerasim's Repose

---

16. "Guardian of Father Herman," in *The Orthodox Word*, no. 29, pp. 223-224.

THE RUGGED COASTLINE OF SPRUCE ISLAND

II

A Visit to Father Gerasim

❦

I VISITED FR. GERASIM on Spruce Island near Kodiak, Alaska, when he had already had 25 years of desert dwelling and was worn out from the unjust suffering inflicted on him for his refusal to adjust himself to church politics; this struggle also undermined his spiritual strength. He lived in a small hut 500 steps from the roaring ocean shore in an extremely thick spruce forest. So dense is this northern jungle that one cannot walk through it save on the laid-out paths. Farther on in the thicket is the chapel built 80 years ago over the grave of St. Herman.

His cell, which he built himself, had a little annex, his bedroom, where he conducted his prayer-rule, and a low closet for firewood near his stove. Everything was neat and orderly to perfection: freshly-painted and often-swept floors, quilted rugs, lace curtains and a bedspread over a hard-board bed, and many inexpensive icons with a number of hanging lamps. I immediately recognized that this excessive tidiness was a means of keeping sanity in this intense loneliness and the overwhelming growth of the wilderness. The coziness was for the sake of warmth but not comfort, which is deadly for a Christian everywhere and always.

VIEWS OF MONKS' LAGOON, SPRUCE ISLAND
as it looked when Fr. Gerasim lived there, 1961.

Like St. Herman he occasionally had to go to take care of his Aleut flock, who lived at the other end of this impenetrable island, but he preferred to stay permanently in his beloved hermitage, caring for St. Herman's grave. There he unfailingly performed all the monastic church services, praying alone for the world, lost in the denseness of the Alaskan wilds.

During the Dormition fast he served akathists in his cell and commemorated *all* the people he had met in his life. The lists were endless, and so were his tears. I was shaken to the depths of my soul at that prayer. I was caught up in the fervency of his pleading, imploring prayer, and I could not help but weep my heart out, as I never had before or after. But the tears were not tears of sorrow, but of some sweet, unexplainable contrition of heart. There before me, in the commemoration of his friends, passed the whole panorama of his life, for I recognized the names of his parents, monks, bishops, Athonites, fellow laborers in the vineyard of Christ in Alaska, and endless names of his spiritual children whom he had baptized, married, and then sung burial services for — many of them lost in the cold waters of the stormy ocean. When he would finish this prayer, he would be cheerful again as usual, offering me tea and salmon pie (*pirog*) of his own baking, and only the starry sky far above the gigantic black spruces bore witness to the length of his *standing before God*. But my heart felt unusually light, and a burning inspiration transfigured all my being.

He told me much during my unforgettable stay with him, about his Kaluga childhood and the Holy Russia he bore in his loving heart, about the Optina elders, his Athonite period, and the early days of apostolic labors in Alaska. He spoke with sobriety and truth and warm sincerity: about the miracles of Sts. Herman and Seraphim that he saw with his own eyes, and his bitter years of persecution. As his "leitmotif" he frequently returned to his deep sorrow: "The love for Christ is abandoning our sinful planet."

His standard was the basic Christianity of the heart. He was a genuine transmitter of the authentic experience of Orthodox Russia, placed in the context of 20th-century America, and yet so few valued him, or simply misunderstood. Most of the clergy who were in contact with him were not guarding the age-old Byzantine worldview as he was, but were men of a "party" mentality who despised him for his straightforwardness. He knew the truth better, he knew that Orthodox truth ever since the Soviet Revolution was destined to be persecuted and thus suffer belittlement or various forms of distortion; he knew well the spirit of the "renovationists." Yet he knew too well that the Truth will make men free, and his conscience commanded him to speak out — and so he spoke, eloquently, to the point, with humbleness of heart, uncomplicated and brief.

While Archimandrite Gerasim is not considered a theologian by those whose concept of theology requires learned homilies and advanced degrees, he is indeed a theologian in the true and ancient sense of the word — one who *knows God*. He knew God not simply through book-knowledge, but by a life of true Christian struggle and prayer. It is precisely this *living* Christianity which ignites the heart and sheds the light of Christ into the darkness of the world.

The days were long and warm, late in August. We took walks together, and he showed me spots of unbelievably abundant ripe salmonberries. I ate to satiety, but he only picked berries and made a pie for me. There he used to meet bears and other wild animals. The craggy shores abounded with multicolored wild flowers . . . and the constant flow of his tales of the saints of old and Russian ascetics involuntarily transported my imagination to St. Herman's Valaam or Fr. Gerasim's beloved Mt. Athos, where he knew and corresponded with many righteous slaves of God.

There also, at the grave of St. Herman, my spiritual life was transformed and a dedication to the cause of St. Herman was born. We spent together the hundredth anniversary of the canonization of St. Tikhon of Zadonsk in solemn all-night vigil. I read to him my seminary thesis on this Saint, which in the tenderness of his heart brought tears to his eyes.

I covered many important subjects with him and I was exposed to a new, indispensible dimension which my seminary education had not covered: what America and our 20th-century world needs is to have a *living link* with the universal Apostolic Tradition, a link which stems from the past and leads to the future, and which no books or learned lectures can give; this is, as it were, the mystical aspect of the apostolic succession.

When I was leaving him, an abandoned, even despised old man standing there in tears alone on the shore of Monks' Lagoon, I knew then that I had beheld, contrary to my expectation, a spiritual giant who breathed into me a *life of decision,* a resolve for a living continuation of St. Herman's work for the glory of God in His Orthodox Church, and that, with God's help, *nothing* could take this away from me.

Abbot Herman
Summer, 1979

The moss-flanked path leading from Monks' Lagoon to Fr. Gerasim's cabin, the Kaluga Mother of God chapel, and the Sts. Sergius and Herman church.

III

Desert Soliloquies on New Valaam

RANDOM TREASURES OF FR. GERASIM'S CONTEMPLATIONS

> *Full many a gem of purest ray serene*
> *The dark unfathom'd caves of ocean bear:*
> *Full many a flower is born to blush unseen*
> *And waste its sweetness on the desert air.*
>
> Thomas Gray

PROLOGUE

EVER SINCE ST. HERMAN OF ALASKA first stepped on the shore of Spruce Island's eastern beach, later known as Monks' Lagoon, the whole area became sanctified for monastic habitation. He came there to seek ascetic solitude, for his soul since childhood had been dedicated to desert living. His excuse to stay on this island was experimental gardening, for originally it was here, as well as on Afognak Island, that the first agricultural work was conducted by the Russian monks with some surprising success (in 1796).

The soul of this Valaam desert-lover found a spot where he

felt best to be "alone with God" even though it cost him much suffering and persecution from the world. And ever since the lure of free monastic soarings became associated with this hallowed spot, so reminiscent of his Old Valaam and so suited in the New World for severe genuine ascetic habitation.

When a century later another truth-loving monk from Holy Russia, Archimandrite Gerasim (1888-1969), about whom St. Herman prophesied, came here to "live for God alone," he potentially realized St. Herman's dream of a monastery on the island. For it was by way of him that various other monks[1] came and went, leaving their spiritual contributions of sweat and tears, like the multicolored stones of a mosaic, upon the poetic panorama of the island which St. Herman bequeathed to all monks of good will.

The historic significance of our Fr. Gerasim, however, rests not so much on the fact that he was an authentic bearer of the best monastic traditions of Holy Russia and that he was a righteous monk in his own right, but rather that his pure, almost child-like, God-loving, forthright soul was free of the weight of ecclesiastical baggage, and his spiritual vision was unobstructed to view life aesthetically. Like any true Orthodox mystic, who flees all aspects of fakery, he perceived God as beauty. — Or, as St. Arsenius the Great would render: "I love all and I flee everyone," in order to behold God's image undistorted. To the contemporary ultra-sophisticated and theologically tired mind, Fr. Gerasim will, most likely, fail to evoke any interest. But to today's rising young generation of God-seekers, so thoroughly confronted with the cosmological nearness of the aeons of star-stuff, of which they themselves are made, the simplicity of Fr. Gerasim cannot but intrigue their souls with the harmonious relationship, without an intermediary, between the creature and its Creator.

As devoted disciples of Fr. Gerasim, we have been gathering for over a quarter of a century these precious little bits and pieces to bring about one whole "icon" of St. Herman's New Valaam. Here

---

1. Such as Schema-Archimandrite Macarius, Fr. Sergius Irtel, and others.

we share them with the humble-hearted reader capable of grasping between the lines the other-worldly beauty of guilelessness in Christ!

Abbot Herman
Spruce Island, Alaska
Meeting of the Lord, 1985

"A Lamp Within the Depth of Night"

A Poem to Fr. Gerasim on Spruce Island

With love and great respect I greet you now —
For draughts of work and prayer you have drunk.
I have but one desire: I wish somehow
The world will know what is, in truth, a monk.

Within Spruce Island's woods there dwelled apart
A godly elder, helpless and in need,
With hopes for New Valaam within his heart:
And there he died — his suffering soul was freed.

The simple, guileless natives did proclaim
This kindly man among the saints to be;
In times of trouble they would call his name,
Believing he would come and hear their plea.

Indeed he came to them. — The path is still
Not overgrown that leads up to his grave.
His life, a humble legend, ever will
Be crowned with glory that the people gave.

And over where he lay, some men erected
An altar with a church and went away;
And to the laws of time it was subjected
Till all was left in dust and in decay.

And, meanwhile, much was written; some proposed
To build a monastery (so they thought).
Troparions, Akathists were composed —
The ruin of the chapel they forgot.

Through storms, in snow, in violent winter weather,
The church was wrecked and lay in disrepair,
Without a caring hand to keep together,
Preserve, protect the holy objects there.

And then, directed by the Higher Power,
You, a true monastic, came and fell
Before the Saint that memorable hour,
And, having prayed, with him you chose to dwell.

None but you, without a friendly word
From those who should have helped you in your plight,
And with no worldly praise or gain procured,
Have lit the lamp within the depth of night.

And now you're weak, with little time to live;
A dream, blown in from Athos, murmurs low.
Your heart, I know, is warm and sensitive
When pangs of gentle sorrow come and go.

Through storms, in snow, in violent winter weather,
The church was wrecked and lay in disrepair,
Without a caring hand to keep together,
Preserve, protect the holy objects there.

With love and great respect I greet you now —
For draughts of work and prayer you have drunk.
I have but one desire: I wish somehow
The world will know what is, in truth, a monk.

by Michael Z. Vinokouroff (Tayazhnik)
January 11/24, 1959, Washington, D.C.

> All these years in my beloved, quiet desert have been dear to me. Every time I pray before the grave of Elder Herman, I thank him that he accepted me, that he took me into his monastery, into his quiet desert....
>
> — Archimandrite Gerasim

1. RESURRECTION OF A SKETE

The time flies swiftly, swiftly flows our earthly life. I again spent more than two weeks in Afognak village and celebrated there my nameday,[2] the 4th of March. I lived in the house of an old lady. In former days, she gave lodgings to Archbishop Vladimir and to Hierarchs Nikolai and Tikhon [Patriarch], and later to Archimandrite Anatole [New Martyr, who became Bishop of Irkutsk], Priest Basil Martyshka, Tikhon Shalamov and others. This is a kind and deeply believing Christian woman, and everyone calls her Babushka Parasceva.

I spent the 4th of March quite festively. On the eve I served an all-night Vigil. The magnification was to St. Gerasim on the Jordan River, and the Akathist was to the Mother of God "Joy and Consolation." After the Vigil, I served a panikhida. That was the day of my mother's repose. She died on the 4th of March, 1920. Of course, this is natural — as there are namedays, so also there are deaths. But my tears flowed through the entire panikhida.

Not long ago, I had the misfortune of falling from a pier into the sea. They pulled me out unconscious. They later told me that I had been remembering my mother all the time. That is why I prayed for her from the bottom of my heart.

. . . But I decided to abandon Afognak, where I lived for 19 years. And tears again. . . . Of course, the new generation is hardhearted and cold. But the old men and women were crying as they bade me farewell. Now I live in the village of Ouzinkie, where I will stay for several weeks. The chapel on the spot where Fr. Herman died is not yet completed. Its size is 14 x 12 feet. It is wooden and its inside is covered by plywood. It has two windows. Everything should be simple there, just as was the humble cell of Fr. Herman. But I will turn it into the Greek "Paraklis": that is, a small chapel without an iconostasis, only a curtain. I will see what can be done. But I am limitlessly happy that my wish has come true,

---

2. Before he became a monk, Fr. Gerasim was named Michael, after St. Michael the Archangel.

Monk's Rock, located between Monks' Lagoon and Kodiak Island. In the background, directly behind the Rock, is Mount Monashka ("Mount Nun").

Fr. Gerasim's cabin (foreground) and the Kaluga Mother of God chapel, as they look today.

that a chapel has already been erected on the spot where for a whole 40 years a bright candle burned, where lived a great righteous man who prayed for the sinful world — Fr. Herman. I want so much to resurrect that which is dear and akin to me, that which is holy, here in this land, when in my native land everything is destroyed. One wishes so much to see this dear skete, a skete that would be filled with prayer near the grave of the holy elder. A skete... O Lord, help!

(May, 1936)

2. FLOWER-COVERED CLIFFS

Today is Sunday, June 6th. I took a walk on the eastern side of the island. The view from the hills of the vastness of the ocean is just beautiful! On the cliffs — right in the cracks of the rocks — grow yellow flowers. Some of the towering rocks are all decorated with them. I looked and thought: to each tiny flower, each blade of grass, the Great Artist indicated a spot where to grow! How wonderful is God's world, God's nature!

(1948)

3. ST. MICHAEL'S DAY

The weather today is wonderful and sunny, and silence reigns. I took a walk and went quite far. The sun shone brightly as I walked; the sea was calm and silent and was not grouchy. In the distance I clearly saw the mountains of Kodiak Island and the strait.

Involuntarily, I remembered my childhood, my home, and the quiet, sunny day of November 8th, the day of my angel, my name-day, when, coming home from Church, I had tea with all kinds of pies. I went for a ride to a lake outside of town.

That was so long ago — more than 40 years have gone by. But today it all came alive, it presented itself so clearly, as if I had just seen it. I remembered everything that was dear to me and I became heartsick, began to long to go home. So painfully I wanted to see my native places, my relatives, friends. But now I don't even know where my relatives are, where my friends are.

The faces of my comrades come to mind:
On separate paths my friends have gone,
For some are dead, and some I'll never find
And each of us apart is drawn.

The evening tonight is wondrous — such a mysterious one! The whole sky is scattered with myriads of stars. — And such a dead silence! This occurs very seldom in Alaska.

The woods are silent, as in death:
No sound the ear can capture
Not even in the fleeting breath
Of wind's consoling rapture.

4. PASCHA ON SPRUCE ISLAND

One Tuesday of the third week of holy Great Lent I returned to my beloved desert from Ouzinkie. I spent Pascha here all alone at the grave of Elder Herman. I cleaned and decorated the whole church beforehand, and everything was beautiful. Many candles and lamps were burning. I served Matins, singing in the middle of the church at the coffin of the Elder, and my soul was overjoyed. I finished serving Liturgy and returned home to my cell at 4 a.m. I also sang the Paschal hymn in my chapel. In my cell everything is so clean, cozy; the lampadas were burning, kulichi (Paschal breads) were on the table, and there were deep red eggs on the green moss. A bouquet of flowers stood on the table as well. They were live flowers, Alaskan flowers! Earlier, I had broken some branches of berry bushes and had put them into a jar of water, and they had blossomed out right in time for Pascha. The little blossoms are just like little pearls and they are covering all the branches. Beautiful! — all the more so because our nature is still fast asleep — there is absolutely no greenness around.

But as for Pascha cheese, I have not seen any for all of the last 27 years. It is impossible to obtain cottage cheese here at this time of the year. Creoles and Aleuts do not even have the slightest idea about it. But I remember it every year. With tears did I send my Paschal greeting to my native Russian people during that wondrous Paschal night. . . .

For me this feast day, this holy night alone clearly speaks of Christ's Resurrection and tells us that the time will come when we all will resurrect and will be eternally singing of the Pascha of Christ. Never is Christ so close to us sinners as during the Great Light-Bearing Paschal Night. But nowhere do people so joyfully, so triumphantly celebrate this feast day as in our Russia.

Thus the Lord allowed me to serve Pascha at the grave of the righteous Elder Herman, which I had been wishfully thinking about all the time. Glory be to God!

> On Pascha day, a skylark played
> And on the airy pathways rode.
> To azure heights he was conveyed;
> He sang a Resurrection ode.
>
> That pristine song was then repeated
> By fields and hills — the woods did sing.
> "Awake, O earth!" they thus entreated,
> "Awake and greet your risen King!"
>
> Awake, O mountain, stream and dale,
> And praise Him with the Seraph bands,
> For death He's made of no avail! —
> Rejoice, you verdant timberlands!
>
> O silver lily, columbine
> And violet, blossom out with awe
> And waft your fragrances divine
> To Him Who's made of love a Law!"

It's midnight now, twelve o'clock! The sea is roaring, although it is quiet, for I cannot hear any wind.

I have no news, because I live alone in the forest.

(1943)

5. CHURCHES IN HOLY RUSSIA

In many of our villages in Russia there were beautiful churches, richly adorned. I love our ancient churches, with their massive walls, vaults and columns. They were built well; everything was solidly done, to last for ages. But there was something special in those massive walls — they were as if alive. They were saturated with the prayer of the Russian people. After all, in those good old days our ancestors knew how to pray to God. For many, many kept all the fast days. In their houses they had whole multitudes of holy icons, lampadas. I loved all of that ancient world; I loved those large living rooms with several holy icons and lamps. In many homes people would keep a perpetually burning lamp. One gets so sad when one remembers Russia, the Bolshevik Russia, where the red dragon has been installed and tortures both the body and soul of the Russian people. Oh, Lord, save it!

I remember a prophetic sermon of Father John Vostorgov: "Weep, Russia!" And he spoke this not long before the Revolution.

Wonderful was that time, when in Russia the church bells were ringing, when God's temples were richly adorned, when whole bonfires of candles were burning before the holy icons, when before the holy reliquaries of the saints of God lamps were twinkling like stars in heaven. I love my land, and I shed tears over it in my solitude.

6. NORTHERN LIGHTS

One Sunday evening in March we witnessed intense northern lights. The light appeared at 9 p.m. and not in the north, as it usually does, but in the east. Its first rays were faint, and they rose quickly across the sky. But after half an hour they became flame-like; the heavens were ablaze with a blood-red dawn! It was a frightful spectacle, as if the whole universe was burning. All the while, in the middle of the sky there stood a white cloud, similar to a huge star — it was as if the sky was opened there. The fiery illumination surrounded the whole sky. The snow looked pink, and the water in the ocean looked red. It was light — all the mountains could be seen.

The northern lights were much brighter and much more intense than those of 1938. Then the light was seen in the whole world.

Many people here were talking: "It again prepares us for something." Of course! There is no repentance evident in the people, even after such a frightening war. On the contrary, people have become worse, wilder, perverse, blaspheming God. . . .

(1948)

7. LAMENTATION OVER CONTEMPORARY MONASTICISM
(A letter to Fr. Panteleimon of Jordanville)

Christ is Risen! Dear Batiushka Father Abbot Panteleimon! Christ is Risen! All the Brethren in the Holy Monastery of the Most Holy Trinity!

Thank you for forwarding to me the letter from Fr. Archimandrite John (of Mount Athos). Thank you for the postcard in which you are all photographed in a meadow. You all look like true Russian monks, in ryassas, with beards and in klobuks. How good it is and pleasant to see! You reminded me of my native holy monastery, my monk friends whose whereabouts only God knows now. For a long, long time I have not received any news from them. Of course, I know that many have gone to the world beyond the grave, have passed to a better life. Yes, nowadays it is better for those who have gone to the world beyond the grave with faith in God! We are enduring horrid times today, and the devil has maliciously armed himself against God and His Christ! With evil the world has risen up against Orthodox monasticism. Now two more bastions have fallen: Pochaev[3] and the wondrous monastery of Valaam.[4] There still remains Holy Athos, but even there the Russian monasticism is dying out. Soon, there too the prayer will become silent for our native Russia, for the whole sinful world, and then one should expect universal catastrophe, the Judgement of God over all.

---

3. See *The Orthodox Word*, No. 3, 1965.
4. See *ibid.*, No. 30, 1970.

I feel so sorry for Mount Athos; what a shame that all our holy and great achievements are perishing there!

From the letter of Fr. Sergius Chetverikov, I see that he is laboring to put together a book called "Valaam Patericon" and a book about the great Elder Schema-Archimandrite Paisius Velichkovsky. This is a holy and good work! It is apparent that Fr. Sergius loves monasticism and is monk-loving, and this is a rarity in our evil times. He also wrote very warmly about Optina Monastery[5] and its elders. All these are my native places, precious ones. The days of my youth, the golden years of my monastic life, were spent there. Optina is in the Kaluga region, where also is the beautiful St. Tikhon's Hermitage.[6] That former beauty of monasteries is now ruined, desecrated.

Several times I read about your holy monastery, and somewhere I saw a photo of it. Do not regret that layfolk do not live in the vicinity of your monastery. They so often are a bother to us monks. In the vicinity of St. Tikhon's Hermitage there was a huge village, and there were thus a lot of temptations for monks. For a monk, it is sweeter to be with God in the desert, farther away from the world, from its temptations. I see that you have beautiful nature around your monastery, a lot of greenery and trees. We had a very damp autumn, winter and now spring. It rains day and night. It is very damp, and I do not feel very good. Pray for me, a sinner. On the 11th of May it will be 28 years of my priesthood — that is, I was ordained on May 11th into the rank of hierodeacon, and on the 12th/25th of October as a hieromonk. The years have flown by so quickly, and now it is already 25 years that I have lived in a foreign land.

I thank you once more, dear Father Archimandrite, for your gift, such a nice gift. I love monasticism and monks, and I grieve much for their fate nowadays. But no one is above God!

Your A. Gerasim
1941

---

5. See *ibid.*, No. 117, 1984.
6. See *ibid.*, No. 91, 1979.

8. FORGET-ME-NOTS

The forget-me-not is the state flower of Alaska. There are many of them on the islands of Kodiak, Afognak, Uganik and on other islands, but they are not on Spruce Island. On Yuyak and Uganik, all the shores of the straits are filled with them. There is even an island not far from Kodiak which is called Forget-me-not Island. What a pity that such a lovely flower is not on Spruce Island! The old-timers used to say that it is true that it is not here. But there were many of them in my home region in Tula and the Kaluga province.

During these 25 years that I've lived here, I have not seen this lovely flower here. After all, Alaska is not that rich with wild flowers, and especially with fragrant ones. The ones here are mostly of blue and purple colors.

No, there is nothing here of what I've seen in the fields and woods of Russia. We do have bluebells here, but they are small, as are the yellow-bells. The violets have no smell. I still remember many of our wild flowers which are not here. Even the wild morning glory is not here. I like it very much — it's a happy, gentle flower. I remember how they grew right in the clay on the high bluffs above our river, and how, on a sunny morning, this little pink flower just poured all over that slope. I remember how I admired them — I loved them.

Oh, how beautiful is our Russia, its wonderful nature!!! How we monks loved to roam in the woods and inhale the aroma of the flowers and the scent of the pine and birch trees! As I wandered in the woods then, how I longed to settle somewhere in the forest and to live in a beautiful clearing! Of course, I was young then, and I hid such thoughts from my friends. But there in the woods, our ascetic saints would come to my mind — their lives in our forests far away from the cities and villages. After all, our St. Tikhon's Hermitage would at times get crowded with outside people during the spring and summer months. Pilgrims by the thousands would visit it.

I now remembered the wonderful past, and I became sad.

Forgive me. It is the evening of the 30th of October. Outside it is quiet and overcast.

(1960)

9. PERSECUTION

Well, already 25 years have gone by of my life in far-away Alaska. I have spent a whole quarter of a century here, and yet the local ruling bishop does not consider me his own clergy. I am for him only the distasteful "Karlovci" clergy.

Well, what can I do about it? I am not ashamed to wear this "dog tag," because I know very well that these "Karlovci" are our hierarchs who lived there [in Karlovci, Yugoslavia] and were true ascetics and confessors of Christ.

They lived in utter poverty, often in sorrow, persecuted by their own and by outsiders. But they bore high the banner of Orthodoxy. They lived there in the same way as did the holy Apostles and their successors in the early centuries of Christianity. Also, they did not walk about then wearing silk outfits, did not ride in carriages and cars, did not live in luxurious homes, but walked on foot and often did not even have a place in which to lay their heads. Yet they had great love towards God and their neighbor.

And in America, too, those in the Sobor of bishops are all deeply believing: all are true monks and are living as they lived in Russia, in Yugoslavia.

It is not shameful also for me, a sinner, to be in the number of such hierarchs [here follows a list of them: Tikhon of San Francisco, Vitaly of Jordanville, John Maximovitch, Averky, Savva, etc.].

I sense a disaster coming here, if the "Platonites" will not repent! Forgive me.

Ever since the second Schism [of 1946], I remained all alone. To the "Platonites" I remained "Karlovci," and to the Sobor of bishops I remained a "Platonite!" When questioned, "Fr. Gerasim, which jurisdiction do you belong to?" I answered to all: "To Christ's jurisdiction!" Yes, according to Christ's commandment I pray for all, I commemorate all. But truly, this Church separation hurts me very much. Mark it, it began way back in 1926. Forgive me for all that I have written.

I have lived 42 years in this damp, cold Alaska. I still experience the same persecution, which the great Elder Herman also went through.

(1958)

10. CHRISTIAN LOVE

Christian love is evaporating from the face of the earth.

(1958)

11. ST. INNOCENT

Today is the commemoration of the Patron of Siberia, St. Innocent of Irkutsk, and also the nameday of the great luminary Innocent, Apostle of Alaska and of all Siberia. I think that on this day there should be served a Liturgy and panikhida in all the Russian churches in America. But, of course, nothing of the sort happens.

12. THE AUTUMN SUN

Today is the first of November (N.S.). The weather is wonderful. The sun brightly shines and the dewdrops, like diamonds, burn on the tiny needles of little spruce trees. But the dear sun now walks low over the horizon and, because of the tall trees, is not seen much. November and December will pass, though, and the sun will again shine brighter and will rise higher. It is only I who grow ever lower towards the earth. . . .

(1941)

13. DORMITION OF THE THEOTOKOS

Our summer was cold, damp and overcast. Now nature is dying. My feathered friends have become quiet and do not sing any longer. They probably are already thinking of leaving this native land of theirs, this summer residence, and of going safely south before the cold settles in.

VIEW FROM MONKS' LAGOON IN WINTER

MOUNT MONASHKA ("MOUNT NUN") – A VIEW FROM SPRUCE ISLAND

I look at this little yellow-green bird and think: who installed in you the thought of flying away south for the winter? Who indicated to you the way there, to you who were born here in Alaska, in this wild northland, to you who are such a little bird?

Does this not indeed tell us that there is, there exists an Intelligent Creator of the universe, the Lord?

I do not love the autumn. I never liked it in Russia from my childhood days. Even in my childhood years I felt like crying with the approach of autumn, when leaves are flying everywhere and the sun shines so sadly.

Living in St. Tikhon's Hermitage, where there were wonderful flower beds and summer flowers of various sorts were blooming everywhere, I used to feel sorry for the flowers, when the cruel frost was killing them and they were dying. But, everything beautiful perishes in its bloom. Such is the fate of all beauty on earth.

I love flowers very much. Mine also bloomed luxuriantly last summer. I beautifully decorated the Shroud for the Dormition of the Most Holy Mother of God with live flowers. On the eve of the 15th, I served the burial service to the Mother of God, all alone. But it was so joyful, so festive to my soul. The church was adorned with greenery. On the Shroud lay a magnificent wreath made from live flowers. I carried the Shroud around the church. I even forgot that I was alone in the church. . . .

Now I guess one could sing:

> Very soon the winter's chill
> Will visit forest, field and glen;
> The flickering light from cabins will
> Appear to shine more brightly then.

Yesterday, September 13th (Aug. 31st), I went to pick mushrooms, and today I'm baking a pie with them. What a pity that you are so far away and cannot share with me my monastic trapeza [meal]! I'm catching fish with my hands — and large ones, too.

(1943)

14. SUMMER IDYLL

In summer, we novices of St. Tikhon's Hermitage in Kaluga would go away to fish, or to bail hay in the wide openness of the Russian fields. That was the happiest time, the healthiest. We slept on the fragrant hay, drank the purest water, and went swimming in the deep river, which was very clear because in the vicinity there were no cities, no factories which polluted many of our rivers. We breathed the clean, sweet-scented air of our fields and forests.

It would also happen that we young novices would sneak out at night and row far away in order to sing some beautiful songs together in a harmonious chorus. As we would be floating in the night we would sing good Russian songs with deep content, or at times would burst out singing church hymns. . . . Oh, that was the most wonderful time, unforgettable time!

(1941)

15. MOON OVER MONKS' LAGOON

Today is October 11th (N. S.). The weather is wonderful, the sun shines so brightly, so warmly. I hauled logs from the shore and got quite tired. Yesterday I read well into the night. And the night was so beautiful, so magical. The moon came out and shone with such melancholy upon our poor little island. I love the moon; I love its sad, silvery light.

> From behind a craggy tower
> Swims the moon into the sky.
> Pensively, with mystic power,
> In the clouds it wanders by.
>
> When Alaskan night's impending,
> I, with restless, sleepless gaze,
> Watch the moon as it is wending
> Through the sky its solemn ways.

And today the waters of the sea are azure blue, just like in summer. I sat on a log of driftwood, admired the beauty of God's world and thought: how wonderful is God's world, what abundance there is of everything in it, what spaciousness all over! But people do not live in unison — they argue, they fight, they shed blood, ruin cities, destroy villages and all that is beautiful, all that is valuable, which was being built up for whole centuries. For what purpose and why? Who will give an answer in this frightful time of war?

(1941)

16. THE DAY OF ST. HERMAN'S REPOSE

Today is November 15/28. I served Liturgy during the night. It was good to pray when it was quiet, peaceful, and when the whole sky was strewn with stars. And involuntarily I thought: probably the same type of night was in 1836 on the 15th of November, when blessed Elder Herman died.

17. BELOVED DESERT

I never sought a rich parish, nor the gaining of more dollars. All these 23 years in my beloved, quiet desert have been dear to me. Every time I pray before the grave of Elder Herman, I thank him that he accepted me, that he took me into his monastery, into his quiet desert. Last summer I served 45 Liturgies there. But now because of ill health I've been detained here, and I miss my desert. Your old Monk Gerasim, the lowest servant of Elder Herman, January 24, 1959.

18. ST. HERMAN BROTHERHOOD

You are doing a good thing organizing a Brotherhood of Saint Herman, Wonderworker of Alaska! May God help you! But keep in mind that Satan does not like such things; he causes evil deeds to those who glorify God's chosen righteous people. I experienced myself the same thing upon my arrival in Alaska. . . . I greet all the brothers. May God and His Most Pure Mother protect you.

(June, 1963)

19. NEW MARTYRS MOSES AND ZOSIMA
of the Meeting of the Lord Skete at St. Tikhon's Monastery

About six miles from St. Tikhon's Monastery [in Russia] there was a skete dedicated to the Meeting of the Lord. But its silence was broken when in its vicinity railroad tracks were laid and a station was built called "St. Tikhon's Hermitage."

There in this skete, monk-ascetics labored for their salvation. One of those living there was Fr. Hieromonk Moses, a monk of holy life practicing silence, a semi-recluse. He was like God's angel in the flesh. A simple monk from a stock of simple, illiterate people, he was intelligent and had the gift of discernment. He was tortured to death by Bolsheviks during the first years of the cruel Revolution. I wrote about him to Fr. Michael Polsky, but for some reason he omitted this in his second volume of *The New Martyrs of Russia*. About Fr. Moses and Fr. Zosima I wrote only what my monk-friends wrote to me from Russia: how they suffered for the name of God. But I also knew them personally when I lived in St. Tikhon's monastery. . . .

Fr. Zosima was a 90 year-old holy elder who was burned alive in his forest cell, where he lived as a forester. He was the kindest elder you could meet. He loved to recall the old times, when everything in the monastery was poor and simple, during his early years. Then all the brethren lived in great mutual friendliness. There was more Christian love amidst the brethren then.

Fr. Zosima was very popular with the young novices. When he would come to the monastery from his far-away forest-ranger's hut, they would all invite him to have tea with them and give them a spiritual talk, which would last until midnight. And this talk was not just idle talk. Oh no, the guileless Elder would tell the young ones what ought to be central for a young novice — obedience. He would narrate many stories from his long life of monastic experience, and this would edify all of them to be kind, obedient.

Already in the first years of the Revolution, Fr. Job wrote about the martyrdom of Elder Zosima:

"We have had new martyrs among us after the overthrow of

the Tsar. Some hooligans tied up Elder Zosima and burned his forest cabin. His burned bones were brought to the monastery. Our brothers were all the time working on the farm, doing the work themselves. In the autumn they began to bring to the monastery whatever was gathered during the summer, and some young hoodlums attacked them and beat them up terribly. Some of them are crippled for life. They did inhuman things to the defenseless monks, tearing out the hair on their heads and beards. . . . And many have already departed to another world." And similar frightful things have occurred all over Russia.

Holy new martyrs of Kaluga, pray to God for us!

20. GREAT MARTYR TSAR NICHOLAS

(A letter to Fr. Gerasim's Father Confessor, Archimandrite Ambrose of Canada)

My life, beginning from childhood years, was very sorrowful. I had to suffer a lot. Much suffering I had to go through, and to endure evil slander. Each of us is carrying his own cross. And beginning from 1914, that terrible year of war, I have suffered in my soul; and since 1917, from the year of that cursed Revolution, I have poured out rivers of bitter tears. Today, on July 3/16, I served Liturgy and remembered the Tsar-Martyr and his family, as if seeing the cellar of the Ipatiev House and that frightful, bloody picture. And I poured out tears and prayed from within myself. Not for the martyrs, no, but for the whole of the Russian people. I begged them, the martyrs, to forgive all of us, to pray for us sinners. Christians of the first ages would glorify and place into the codex of martyrs all those who were killed for Christ; and they prayed not *for* them, no, but *to* them — to those who suffered for Christ. But these were four innocent Princesses and the young Crown Prince Alexis. And they all suffered for eighteen months from crude, vicious and filthy guards. They all are: Great Martyrs. And also the great Grand-Duchess Elizabeth was a wonderful woman! Yes, indeed, a righteous one of the twentieth century! . . .

TSAR-MARTYR NICHOLAS II

An enlargement of a small photograph treasured by Fr. Gerasim at Monks' Lagoon.

And my poor Aleuts think of nothing except drinking and carousing....

A frightful night is approaching, and I will serve Matins. Millions of Orthodox Russian people have not defended their kind, meek Tsar and his family! It is frightful to think what took place there that night; and it is no less frightful that against the Tsar were also some hierarchs, priests and educated monks. Of the simple people all, I think, were for the Tsar. But no, there were also some of them who were revolutionaries. I served Matins for the repose of their souls and a great panikhida. I grow very tired.

All day I am on my feet, and I sleep badly. I thank the nuns that they worry about me. I do not forget them. I pray for them. The time flies so fast. August will soon be here and after that the stormy autumn. It appears that I will not have time to live in a nice, warm place. Oh, how I painfully remember St. Tikhon's Monastery. On the 16th of June I decorated with beautiful flowers the whole chapel and served a complete vigil service to the Saint. I even read and sang stichera as a canonarch — all alone. Of course, I felt sorrow and missed my dear brotherhood. Occasionally I write to Archbishop Averky.

(July, 1960)

I remember a dream I had of the Emperor which I saw at the time of my deep sorrows, when spiteful bishops and slandering priests persecuted me and with malice judged me. The Emperor said to me at that time: "I understand you. I myself endured all this," and his eyes became very sorrowful.

(March 7, 1963)

21. CHILDREN OF ONE MOTHER

I cannot sleep well; I sleep little. And if it happens that I wake up, then I take the prayer rope and begin to pray for all the reposed ones. I commemorate them at the Proskomedia [for the Divine Liturgy]. Just think, this is the bloodless sacrifice offered for the sins of all the dead from the beginning of the world. Fr. Roman Sturmer commemorates at Proskomedia only those who belong to the Platonite jurisdiction. No, not me. I commemorate *all*. We are all children of the same mother, the Orthodox Church; all children of one mother, Holy Russia. And how terrible are these church divisions!!! But this goes on today everywhere.

(June, 1965)

22. DIVINE FRAGRANCE

May the mercy of God be with you. Forgive me for my long silence. I left the desert on the 23rd of September, and of course — as each time — with pain of heart. The terrible earthquake has not straightened us out, nor has it brought us to repentance. And this takes place not only in Alaska, but throughout the whole world. Sad! I'm already a 76 year-old man, and it's high time for me to retire to a cell.

I received the book on Elder Schema-Archimandrite Gabriel, and as soon as I received it I read it through several times. Forgive me, but I cannot understand how it could have happened that Fr. Gabriel decided to abandon Optina Monastery, that "spiritual hospital" of Russian believing people, and how, having lived there for five years, he ran to the noisy city of Moscow. I remember how Hierarch Theophan the Recluse wrote to one hieromonk who wanted to visit Moscow: "Moscow sweeps you off your monastic feet." It's apparent from this that the righteous Hierarch did not particularly wish for a monk to linger in our noisy capital.

Besides this, the fragrant aroma in the cell of Fr. Gabriel was mentioned in the book as being similar to perfume, which is invented by people. The paradisal aroma, however, as sensed by many of our holy people (ascetics) is in no way reminiscent of perfume, even the most expensive ones.

In 1926, on the 14/27 of May, when I visited the desert hermitage of Elder Fr. Herman, praying on the spot of his blessed repose where a little chapel has now been built, and when I exclaimed, "Christ is Risen, Batiushka Fr. Herman!" I was surrounded by a strong aroma. It was more similar to fragrant incense from Mount Athos, but in no way to those perfumes which are sold all over the world. This was the second time such a thing occurred to me in my life.

In St. Tikhon's Monastery, at the end of January, 1907, Hierodeacon Jerome reposed. He had a chronic epileptic sickness with seizures. One evening he went to light a lamp in the corridor with a wax candle stub. In the corridor of the infirmary (where he worked) he fell down and his hair caught fire, as well as his rather solid beard. The candle was burning on his chest, and his cassock and under garments were burned.

Since there were no sick people upstairs [in the infirmary], I had gone to the icon-making shop, where we mounted paper icons on boards and covered them with glass and tin frames. I came to the infirmary around 5:00 in the evening. As I entered, I smelled in the corridor the terrible odor of burnt wool. I quickly unlocked my cell and lit the lamp; and then I could see a man entering it whose voice was that of Fr. Jerome, but there was no beard and no hair. That was a frightful sight!! This was in December of 1906. Having suffered in pain for about a month, Fr. Hierodeacon Jerome died. Before his death he accepted the schema. His repose was blessed. Before dying he parted with me, promising to pray for me if the Lord would vouchsafe him blessed life after death.

In June of 1907 I had a dream in which, walking to the Transfiguration Cathedral, I saw Schema-hierodeacon Jerome standing near his grave, in mantle and klobuk. He looked so young, approximately thirty years old; and everything he wore was brand new. That same day, at about 5:00 in the evening, as I was approaching the door of my cell, I was suddenly surrounded by a wonderful aroma. Really, it felt just as if someone had censed with fragrant Athonite incense. I looked around at the cells, but they were all locked up. The elders had gone to church, and the infirmarian, Fr. Myron, was downstairs in the pharmacy.

I told my elder, Schemamonk Ioasaph, about this. Having heard me out, he answered: "Misha, you told me that Fr. Jerome promised to pray for you if the Lord would vouchsafe him blessed life. And here, if you would not have been afraid, he would have appeared to you in a vision, since things like that used to happen and are still happening. But you are a nervous one, and therefore he could not appear to you visually. But his soul visited you. This fragrance let you know that he is in a blissful state in the heavenly abodes and is praying for you...."

Yes, that fragrant aroma that I sensed near the door of my cell is impossible to compare to any perfume, even the most expensive ones. This is what I cannot understand in the life of Elder Gabriel.

(December, 1964)

23. ST. SERAPHIM

No, I rarely think about gaining dollars. Glory be to God, so far I have had no lack of a piece of bread and a cup of tea; we here have not experienced that which our people have endured in Russia for these forty-three years. No, we haven't! In the eighth Ikos of the Akathist of the "Joy of All Who Sorrow," I love these words: "Our whole life on earth is filled with sickness and sorrow from slanders, regret, reproach and multi-faceted tribulations and calamities!" Or in the seventh Kontakion: "We're all pilgrims and travellers on this earth," and in the words of the Apostle, "Sorrows from enemies, sorrows from relatives, sorrows from false brothers, in deprivations and dissatisfactions...."[7]

And this evening I sang this. I also love St. Seraphim the wondrous elder, as well as St. Ephraim the Syrian. And I often think of how much harder our life would be if we didn't have holy men and women of prayer, the saints. Oh, how close they are to us when we, with faith and love, run to them. And what consolation St. Seraphim left to those who loved him: "When I will be no longer, come to me, to my grave; come whenever you have time, and the more often the better. And whatever is on your soul and whatever burden you have or whatever will happen to you, come and bring it to me, so that when you fall to the earth as to one living, I will hear you and your sorrow will disappear. And as to one living, speak to me and I will be for you always alive." Yes, indeed. This, for those who

---

7. *Cf.* II Cor. 11:26-27.

love Batiushka Seraphim, is a great consolation!!! I believe that in Soviet Russia there are still many who love and venerate St. Seraphim. I heard that they frequent his desert hermitage. They come secretly and carry away either a little pine cone or a little bit of earth. . . .

Today I have peace in my soul. I served Liturgy with joy, and it is so quiet. And the weather is so beautiful. I had visitors, and they were all very kind and cheerful. And last night the wonderful moon enlightened my whole desert forest. But today the skies are overcast by clouds. The days pass so quickly. It is already autumn, and in the morning the air is already cold. . . .

It is raining. Fog. There is no mail from Kodiak. I am sitting at home, I don't feel too well, and my feet feel so heavy. I do not know what awaits me in the future. May the will of God be upon everything. I believe that my heavenly friends — St. Seraphim of Sarov, St. Herman of Alaska and others — will not abandon me. . . .

I love my desert. To me it is the most sacred place in the world. But in such old age it is hard for me to spend winters there.

(October, 1964)

24. A MIRACLE OF ST. SERAPHIM

Upon my arrival in Alaska I began to glorify St. Seraphim of Sarov. When I lived in Afognak, Alaska, there was a Creole, Theodotus Grigoriev, who had a hernia. Once, as he was lifting his boat, a "pinching of his hernia" occurred. I was called to him and saw him suffering terribly. From a doctor's manual I found out that the hernia could not get back into its place, and the man (I don't remember now after what period of time) would die in terrible pain. But this man had a wife, a large family — a whole bunch of children, and an old mother, a very nice grandmother. But I also knew that St. Seraphim loved children, and I began to pray to him to have mercy upon the sick man because of his children. And what happened? I heard that his hernia quickly entered into its place. On the next day, when I came to visit him and he began to thank me, I told him: "Do not thank me, but thank St. Seraphim. I asked his help. I will come back and we shall serve him a thanksgiving moleben service. Before this Theodotus used to drink, but after his healing he became sober. Now he is no longer alive; he died as a Christian should. Yes, "Wondrous is God in His saints, the God of Israel." I am sending my donation for the needs of the Brotherhood, in the name of Elder Herman...

The blizzard howls ferociously. I am thinking of the little birds. It must be cold for them.

(February, 1963)

25. BLESSED JOHN

Blessed was the death of the hierarch, Archbishop John [Maximovitch]. It is sad to see going to the other world — in such a troubled, terrible time as ours — such luminaries of Christ's Church!

I remember how, still in Russia, our good believing people used to say, when our righteous ones, luminaries, would die: "Evidently something terrible will occur in Russia, since the Lord calls to Himself righteous people of prayer." Yes, that's how it is: righteous ones are passing away, and there are no chosen ones of God to replace them.

(1966)

Fr. Gerasim in his old age in Kodiak.
From the collection of Gene Sundberg.

IV

Man's Heavenly Friends

by ARCHIMANDRITE GERASIM

IN THE SPIRITUAL JOURNAL "Spiritual Seminar," which was sent to me from Harbin, I read a wonderful article, "Man's Heavenly Friends." Involuntarily I felt contrition of heart from all that was written by the respectful author of this truthful article, I. Kostuchik. It is true that we are not alone, that our heavenly protectors are ever with us no matter where we are.

I was still young when I began to think of monastic life, even though as a child I had not seen any monasteries. In 1905 I timidly drew near my sick father's bedside and said, "Papa, bless me to enter a monastery." My ailing father asked for an icon and blessed me for the monastic life with an icon of St. Tikhon of Zadonsk. I was dreaming then of entering the Shcheglov Nativity Monastery which was located near the noisy city of Tula. At that time, there lived and labored for salvation a clairvoyant Elder, Hiero-schema-monk Dometian, who told me: "The Lord Himself will show you the path." I did not enter Shcheglov Monastery then but returned home. However, in July of 1906, we walked on a pilgrimage to the St. Tikhon of Kaluga desert monastery as a whole group.

Having reached the holy monastery of St. Tikhon and seeing its beautiful temples, the beauty of its belfry, the wonderful nature, I was overjoyed and my lips repeated: "This is God's paradise on earth!" Deciding to remain and live there, I went to Fr. Archimandrite, who listened to me and briefly explained the difficulties of monastic life: that one must be obedient, humble, rise early for Matins, etc. Then he rose from his chair and led me to an artistically executed painting which depicted the mother of St. Tikhon of Zadonsk, leading him as a young boy to town to give him away to a coachman; his elder brother was shown standing on his knees in the dusty road, imploring his mother to give "Timosha" to the spiritual school. Pointing to the picture, the Archimandrite told me: "Here the mother of Hierarch Tikhon wanted to give him over to the care of a coachman, but the older brother overtook her on the road, threw himself down at her feet and said, 'Mother, don't take Timosha to be brought up by a coachman. Give him to a coachman and he will become a coachman. Better for us to give him away to a spiritual school and then he'll turn out to be a priest.' You should likewise try to lead a God-pleasing life," said the Abbot, "and you'll also become a monk." He was silent for a moment, then said with a smile, "and perhaps even an archimandrite." It so happened that for a time I was Archimandrite Laurence's cell-attendant; and in cleaning his room I often stood admiring that picture, which became very dear to me. In 1911 I went to Mt. Athos, to where my soul was yearning and about which I had read a lot. In 1912 I returned to Russia but did not return any longer to my St. Tikhon's Monastery; I remained instead in Tula, in the metochion of the Protection of the Most Holy Theotokos, which was being built then by Bishop Evdokim Meschersky. Bishop Evdokim, at that time, was a wonderful hierarch; he loved solemn services and loved to give sermons on the word of God. I began to live there quietly and peacefully under the protection of the Most Holy Mother of God, and the busy city did not bother me in the least. The Bishop built there a majestic cathedral. The people of Tula were good and religious, and generously contributed to the adornment of the temple of God. My obedience was my most favorite of all the obediences — I worked in the church as a candle lighter and sacristan. The church was huge, there was a lot of work, and I was alone to do it. Very often Bishop Evdokim

ARCHIMANDRITE LAURENCE
of the St. Tikhon of Kaluga Monastery

would say to me: "Poor Michael, you are tired! But endure a little longer and soon I will tonsure you, and you will be a monk." The Bishop was telling me that he would tonsure me, with all solemnity, and that he would summon many of the monastery monks. In my soul I was against this because I remembered how the monastic tonsure was performed in St. Tikhon's Monastery, where everything was touching and contrite unto tears. But I was silent and would not answer anything to the Bishop. From all that the Bishop was telling me, nothing came into reality. In 1914 he was appointed to America and he told me: "Michael, come with me to America. At first we will go to Petrograd, where I shall tonsure you and raise you into the rank of hierodeacon." But this, too, did not come to pass. But what did take place was something pleasing to the Lord God and His Saint, the holy Tikhon of Zadonsk. I was tonsured into monasticism by **Bishop Alexander Nyemolovsky** in the Monastery of St. Tikhon of Zadonsk in America on the 24th of April, 1915 (O.S.). Everything there, at that time, was poor and humble, from the Bishop's vestments right down to the singing. Bishop Alexander turned to me with a brief word, "You have lived in prosperous monasteries and worked in rich churches, but the Lord vouchsafed that you be tonsured in such poverty and humbleness. Never forget that St. Tikhon loved this very poverty and he is the protector of this monastery." What does this mean if not that St. Tikhon, that great wonderworker, had taken me into his protection from that very day in which I had devoted myself to the monastic life? My father blessed me with an icon of St. Tikhon of Zadonsk to enter the monastic path; Archimandrite Laurence, in the St. Tikhon of Kaluga Monastery, indicated to me to take St. Tikhon of Zadonsk as an example for me to follow; and I was tonsured in the Monastery of St. Tikhon of Zadonsk, but that is not all yet.

In 1935 I moved to Spruce Island, where the monk-missionary and ascetic, Monk Herman, saved his soul; there he reposed in 1836. In 1936, in the month of July, I cleaned up the whole church and painted it. When all was finished I took home to my cell, to clean and repair, two icons: St. Tikhon of Zadonsk and St. Seraphim of Sarov. I cleaned them up, placed them in new frames and put them in my cell so they would dry out. After finishing the work, I sat down and, looking at the holy faces of the pleasers-of-God, dear to me, my whole life and all that I had endured during all these years emerged before me. Then, suddenly, I remembered: Why, it was on this very day today, on the 17th of July, that I entered the monastery. And I remembered clearly: from that day, the 17th of July, in 1936, a full thirty years of my monastic life had transpired.

Tears involuntarily rolled down my face; I got down on my knees and, kissing the holy icons, I said, "God's beloved, you are my dear guests; and you came to me, a sinner, on the very day I entered the monastery." I had a special veneration and love for these very saints: St. Tikhon of Zadonsk and the wondrous St. Seraphim of Sarov.

And how well it was said; how truly did I. Kostuchik, in his article, call the angels of God and holy God-pleasers and saints "man's heavenly friends." This is a holy truth!!!

I must also add this, that we monks never forget our heavenly protector, the name of God's angel or God-pleaser who was given to each person at his holy baptism.

I remember that each newly-tonsured monk, after his tonsure, would order to have an icon painted for himself upon which two God-pleasers would be depicted: the Saint who was given to him at baptism and the God-pleaser who was given him at tonsure. And to them the monk prays as to his heavenly protectors.

I cannot be silent also about what took place in 1904, how the Mother of God saved all of us from a fire. At that time, I had a job as a typesetter in the Shebarov print shop. Mr. Shebarov was a reveller, and he and his whole family were atheists. Because of his debts, his printshop was under surveillance; and we worked there daily, deep into the night, putting the type away. One spring night in 1904, there was a terrible rain storm and we all decided to spend the night in the print shop. It was raining heavily outside and we all — six people — lay down in the book bindery on the floor which was covered with cuttings from the books and other waste paper. In the corner of the room there hung an icon of the Mother of

God "Joy of All Who Sorrow," in an old icon case. And, before it, there was a lamp screwed onto it. I decided to light the lamp before lying down and so I poured in oil (I do not know what kind of oil) and lit it. We all lay down on the floor on the cut paper and soon fell asleep. Then, suddenly, I clearly felt that someone strongly shoved me on my side. (Here I must say that in my younger days I used to sleep so soundly that alarm clocks were not able to wake me up.) I woke up and was amazed: before the holy icon there was a huge flame of fire that reached the very ceiling. I grabbed something and covered the fire, and the room at once became very dark. Had the lamp glass broken, then the paper would have caught on fire and there would have been no salvation — for the floor was covered with thick oil from the printing presses and the huge two-storey house was all made out of logs. The whole first floor was occupied by the print shop and book bindery, and on the second floor lived the family of A. P. Shebarov. For a long time I could not come to myself because I clearly saw a miracle from the holy icon of the Mother of God "Joy of All Who Sorrow." I clearly remember, even up to today, that somebody with force and insistence was waking me up — even as my mother used to do when I would have to go to school. It is not my imagination but a holy truth, and I know that the Holy Mother of God saved us from an unavoidable disaster. Loving the flickering of a holy fire, the bright lamp near the icons, I had lit it before going to sleep. We did not fall asleep right away for we talked for a long time; but it was he who lit the lamp of the icon of the Mother of God "Joy of All Who Sorrow" who was awakened.

Yes, it is holy truth that we are not alone in this earthly life, that we have heavenly protectors and defenders, as I have experienced in my life's path. In our frightful time of godlessness, even Orthodox Russian people have become sort of embarrassed to have holy icons in their homes and to light vigil lamps before them. I have seen this for myself when I was in the States among my own Russian people. Involuntarily, I recall my childhood days, that golden time of life, when in each Russian house the main adornments were the icons, before which lamps were burning. I loved these homes; I loved to look at the array of icons, like whole iconostases, with the flickering lights of the burning lamps in front of them. When people rejoiced in decorating their homes with icons, when they kept vigil lamps burning and observed holy feast days, then they lived quietly, peacefully and piously. Each home, each family, was precisely what St. Paul referred to as a house-church. But when the soul of the Russian Orthodox Christian became infected with new fads, he became ashamed of having icons in the home and of lighting before them the holy fire — lampadas. Then a gloomy darkness spread over his soul, causing him to unrestrainedly join the side of the enemies of our Lord Jesus Christ and of everything that is good and holy; and he began to do all that is unheard of, even among wild animals.

And this is why contemporary people do not see miracles performed by the Lord and His saints: because they are spiritually blind and have risen against the Lord and His Church here on earth. Of course, mankind's heavenly friends stand far removed from such people. And man, living next to them, cannot even see or feel them because his sinful state of soul has neither peace nor love. And so, Orthodox Russian Christians, preserve your faith in God. Acquire love for God and for your loved ones, and you will clearly feel that you have in the spiritual world friends and prayerful intercessors before the Lord God. Amen.

Archimandrite Gerasim
Spruce Island, Alaska
June, 1940

Translated from Khleb Nebesny (Heavenly Bread),
Harbin, 1940, no. 6.

SAINT TIKHON OF KALUGA

Commemorated June 16 (†1492)

TROPARION, TONE 4

As a most bright luminary wast thou made manifest in the Russian land,* O our holy Father Tikhon:* thou didst settle in the wilderness,* and leading there a strict way of life, thou didst dwell like a fleshless one,* wherefore God did enrich thee with the gift of miracles.* And so we, hastening to the shrine of thy relics,* say in contrition:* O holy Father,* entreat Christ God that our souls may be saved.

V

St. Tikhon of Kaluga and His Monastery

by ARCHIMANDRITE GERASIM

THE HOLY ABBOT TIKHON OF KALUGA embraced monasticism in his youthful days in Moscow, then he labored for many years in a forest in the hollow of a huge oak near the town of Medin in the Kaluga province. He founded a monastery on that very spot dedicated to the Dormition of the Mother of God, and he was its abbot. St. Tikhon died on June 16, 1492. His holy relics at first were openly exposed in the monastery's main cathedral. But, due to frequent raids on the monastery and the monastery's final destruction, the monks buried the holy relics in the earth where they remained until the time of the Russian revolution. In time, on the spot where St. Tikhon was buried, the magnificent Cathedral of the Transfiguration was erected with five altars, and over his very grave was built an artistically designed reliquary, on which there was placed a large icon of St. Tikhon. A large canopy was constructed over the reliquary, three sides of which were adorned with silver hanging lampadas. The reliquary was located on the right side of the cathedral near the kliros of the main Transfiguration altar. The inside of the five-domed cathedral had a marble-like finish, and was decorated in a rich and ornate manner. Not long before the revolution, St. Tikhon's Monastery, which had retained the title of a desert hermitage, "blossomed like a lily" and was one of the best established of all desert monasteries. There were two magnificent cathedrals in the monastery, that of the Transfiguration, which was the winter church, and a new, beautiful summer cathedral dedicated to the Dormition of the Mother of God. There was erected an elegant belfry with huge bells. In 1906 they hung a new immense bell that weighed 32 tons which could be heard far away in the villages, towns and ranches. In 1909 a large refectory with a church dedicated to St. Nicholas was consecrated. There was another large church near the monastery infirmary. The monastery had many monastic structures, including three guest houses outside the monastery wall. About two miles from the monastery was the spring of St. Tikhon, a church, two separate enclosed pools built into the healing well, one for men and the other for women, and two houses where the monastic brotherhood, consisting of seven or eight monks, lived at that time.

Eight miles from the monastery was a skete dedicated to the Meeting of the Lord, inhabited by thirty monks. In the skete the humble and quiet brotherhood spent its time in hard ascetic labors. The skete was located deep in the forest, and only later did the sound of the railroad tracks which were constructed nearby disrupt the quietness of this wondrous spot in one of the most picturesque areas of the Kaluga region.

God granted me to live in St. Tikhon's Monastery for about six years, becoming well-acquainted with the entire expanse of the monastery. Before the First World War there were 250 brothers in the monastery. The monastery owned much land, many farms and a well-constructed house (metochion) in Kaluga. It is not true, as the Bolsheviks wrote, that the monastery had millions of roubles, and that all the money was lost, having supposedly been deposited in German banks. There was nothing of the sort! I knew the last three of the monastery's archimandrites, Moses, Laurence and Platon, and I knew well that they were true monks, patriotic sons of their Mother Russia. They were all of peasant stock and were far from being so cunning as to send the monastery capital overseas. This is a lie, a slander of the godless ones upon monasticism. I know well that the monastery had a lot of land and a lot of income from this land, but with this the monastery would help many people. There was not a set price for pilgrims to stay in the guesthouse; they would donate whatever they could. All poor people were fed and given lodging free of charge. Everyone would receive rye bread and kvas. The monastery infirmary was open to lay people, and all local peasants and farmers who lived in the vicinity of the monastery. Medical assistance and medicines were given free of charge. In April, 1908, there was a frightful flood throughout all of Russia. This occurred also in the Kaluga region where many villages were washed away by the water. The monastery rendered assistance in every way possible to those who had suffered. The monastery also operated a school for village boys out of which the boys were later able to become teachers and businessmen or take up other professions. I cannot recount all the charitable things the monastery did.

Orthodox Russian people loved St. Tikhon's monastery very much, and hundreds of thousands would visit it every summer. Many of our hierarchs would visit there, too. In the fall of 1911 the monastery was visited by the righteous one of the twentieth century, the Grand Duchess Elizabeth Feodorovna. Kaluga bishops visited the monastery every year on the sixteenth of June, the feast day of St. Tikhon. Bishop Nikodim, Vicar of the Kursk Diocese (of Belgorod), also greatly loved to frequently visit St. Tikhon's Monastery. It was he who was later martyred by the Bolsheviks in 1918. All the monks loved this humble, meek and kind hierarch of God, Nikodim, and would say: "Fortunate indeed will be that diocese which will have as its head Bishop Nikodim."

St. Tikhon was a great miracle worker. From all corners of the wide Russian land people would gather at his grave. There were many miracles which took place at the shrine of his relics and also at his well. Even during my stay there the Lord worked great miracles at his relics and at the spring. A twelve-year-old paralyzed peasant girl who was carried there in her mother's arms was miraculously healed. During the *moleben*,[1] when the hieromonk placed the

---

1. A supplicatory prayer for the living.

Holy Gospel on the head of the sick girl, she stood on her feet and loudly exclaimed: "Mother! Mother, I can walk! I am now healthy." Everyone in the church saw the miracle and wept. Many newspapers wrote about this miracle.

Here is another great miracle which I shall never forget. I do not remember the exact year, but the details of that miracle I well recall. During the days of Great Lent there was brought to the monastery a sick young girl whose arms and legs were paralyzed. She had to be wheeled around the church. Pascha was late that year. It was warm and green everywhere. On the third day after Pascha the sick girl was brought to the spring of St. Tikhon; and the women, having placed her on a sheet, immersed her into the cold, running spring water. And what do you think happened? The girl, already condemned by the luminaries of the medical sciences, stood up on her legs and by herself came out of the water. In 1914, on the eve of April, I myself saw her in one of the convents absolutely healthy, rosy-cheeked and working in the garden. In gratitude for her healing she dedicated her whole life to the service of God by joining the ranks of monastics. There were also a great multitude of other miracles. I was the cell-attendant of the Archimandrite, and I know for sure that people would write; some would ask for holy water, holy oil, and *prosphoras*,[2] while others would ask that a vigil or moleben would be served to Saint Tikhon. During the summertime the requested vigils to St. Tikhon would be held quite often; but then 1918 arrived and the beautiful monastery of St. Tikhon was taken over and defiled by the godless ones. The monks were forced to leave, the holy things were desecrated, the bells and crosses taken down. It is difficult for me even to remember that. My tears do not allow me to write.

St. Tikhon was highly revered by the pious Muscovites, who considered him their own saint because "he embraced monasticism in the city of Moscow." He was also highly revered in our northern capital, the city of St. Peter; for in the grounds of his monastery many residents of St. Petersburg found their eternal rest. In the

---

2. Leavened bread for use in the Divine Liturgy.

basement church of the Transfiguration Cathedral there were many dignitaries buried who spent the last days of their lives inside the walls of the holy monastery. The former governor of Alaska, Simeon Ivanovich Yanovsky, and his son, Hiero-schemamonk Christopher, were buried there. Many were buried around the Transfiguration Cathedral. Before the bloody revolution, on the monastery grounds there was order and cleanliness. The graves were taken care of, and over many of them there were beautiful memorial stones and burning lampadas. And then came the red beast, that terrible, bloody dragon to the Russian land, and he destroyed and defiled everything.

But it is not the first time that the holy monastery of St. Tikhon was destroyed. In the past, its church buildings and walls were destroyed. It seemed that there would never be anything there again. But then the terrible times would pass and the Lord would cleanse Holy Russia from all impurity, and again the holy places of Russia would be resurrected; and just as other monasteries were, St. Tikhon's Monastery would become an oasis in the desert wasteland. Again it would rise from the stubble and ashes, and it would become like other Russian monasteries, a seedbed of enlightenment, a spiritual school of Orthodox culture. The disciples of the holy fathers would settle at the ruins; they would clean up the holy place and once again build temples of God and all that is necessary to sustain the life of man.

One wants to believe that the time will come when, on the Russian land, will shine again the bright Sun of Christian Love, Christian Peace and Christian Brotherhood, when again the temples of God will be reopened, the lamps under its vaults will burn again like bonfires of candles. Then the monks, and with them all Orthodox people will sing, "Rejoice and be glad, O holy and God-pleasing Desert who has nurtured our praiseworthy father, Tikhon." So be it, so be it.

Archimandrite Gerasim
Spruce Island, Alaska

Translated from Pravoslavny Blagovestnik, *San Francisco, January, 1943.*

THE RUSSIAN SKETE OF ST. ANDREW ON MOUNT ATHOS
at the time Fr. Gerasim stayed there.

VI

Is There Life Beyond the Grave?

by ARCHIMANDRITE GERASIM

EDITOR'S NOTE

The following article is of value for many reasons. It expresses in every line the simple, straightforward and guileless Orthodox piety that is so needed today, instilling in the God-fearing reader a desire to prepare himself for the future life. Further, it provides insights into the life of a 20th-century ascetic and confessor, Archimandrite Gerasim. Because Fr. Gerasim was such a dedicated man of prayer, he had mystical contact with several of his close ones who lived far away. They made themselves known to him after they had departed this life, and in many cases this could only have been because they were made to realize the efficacy of his holy supplications before God.

IS THERE LIFE BEYOND THE GRAVE? This question has interested and still interests all nations in all times. Many, very many contemporary "wise" men deny the immortality of the soul, eternal life beyond the grave.

But I would like to share with the reader of spiritual journals how my friends used to inform me about their passing into the other world. I will write the full truth, with no trace of imagination or any form of lies.

1.

I don't remember now the exact year, but it was in 1907-1908, when I was a novice at the St. Tikhon of Kaluga Monastery [in Russia]. One beautiful summer we novices worked together to gather hay about seven miles from the monastery, and we all slept on the fragrant hay in a huge barn that had been specially built to store the hay. One morning at about three o'clock I saw in my dream an old acquaintance of mine, an old lady, who cheerfully greeted me at the porch of our house and said to me, "I don't live here anymore; I live now by myself." But I must say that she lived in Moscow all her life, except that every year she would come to spend the summer with my aunt for about two months. She also came that particular summer, became sick and died in the house of my aunt, with whom she had been a friend for more than forty years.

I woke up feeling a certain sadness, and this sadness would not leave me that whole day. By late evening a monk from the monastery, Fr. Jerome, came and brought mail for all of us monks. I also received a letter, and, opening it, I read: "At 3:00 a.m. Alexandra Alexandrovna died. Pray for her. She used to love you and in dying she remembered you." My dream had turned out to be prophetic, precisely because at that very hour slave of God Alexandra had passed away.

2.

In 1911 I went to Mount Athos and decided to remain there forever, entering the novitiate in the Brotherhood of St. Andrew's Russian Skete. Once I saw in my dream Monk Christopher from my St. Tikhon's Monastery, who had died on the 11th of January, 1911. I saw him walking on a green meadow. The sun was brightly shining all over. Having caught up with me, Fr. Christopher said to me, "Greetings, Father!" And then he added, "You should leave this place, and as soon as possible." I asked him, "Where do you live now, Fr. Christopher?" "Same place — there in St. Tikhon's Monastery," he answered. Then we turned east, and I saw as if the whole of

St. Tikhon's Monastery was placed on a green meadow bathed in sunlight. It was such a beauty: all was blindingly white; the crosses, as if pure gold, were brightly burning on the majestic cathedral and belfry. Then Fr. Christopher led me to the Transfiguration Catholicon, where the relics of St. Tikhon were treasured under the reliquary eaves. I was amazed at its beauty and the luxury of its decoration. Fr. Christopher was a great ascetic. His main virtues were that he never judged anyone and never visited anyone, knowing only the temple of God and his humble cell. I woke up and began to think of what I had seen in my dream.

I had known Fr. Christopher very well; he used to love me. Involuntarily I began to wonder about the dream I had seen and decided to leave not only Mount Athos but even the Athonite Metochion in Odessa, to which I had been appointed to do my obedience. My monk friends called me to go to Tula, to the Protection of the Mother of God city monastery, where there was a dire need for working monks. In 1912, right on the Feast of the Protection of the Mother of God, I arrived in Tula and began to live a quiet life working in the temple. And what transpired meanwhile on Mount Athos? A frightful storm broke out there, evoked by some fanatic monks who, not having a thorough understanding of Holy Scripture, became the "Name-worshippers." And of course, if I had been living on Mount Athos, God knows what would have happened to me at that time. But my wonderful elder, Fr. Christopher, had sternly ordered me to leave that place, and had even hastened me to do it. How amazing! — He was dead at that time, his body lay in damp earth. Who at that time could have warned me to avoid such misfortune? Unquestionably, of course, the immortal soul of Fr. Christopher.

3.

Once while in Alaska (I don't remember the year) at the end of September, I saw in a dream how I drove up to my home and approaching the garden gate, saw my Uncle Valentin (my father's brother). I was very happy to see him; but then I saw that he passed by, pointing with his hand in the direction of the city cemetery and saying to me, "I do not live here anymore. I am going there." I woke up and at once thought: Uncle Valentin probably died. Then I wrote a letter to Russia to his sister Olga and my aunt, describing my dream in detail, the day and the month. And what do you think? My aunt wrote to me in this way: "Your dream did not lie to you: Uncle Valentin died precisely on September 30th in the morning." And again the immortal soul of my uncle informed me, who lived in far away Alaska, about its passing into the other world.

4.

In my childhood and the years of my youth I had a friendly acquaintance with a family that consisted of seven daughters and a son. The family, although poor, was honest and work-loving. The head of the family, Gregory A. Novikov, and his devoted wife worked hard in order to provide an education for their children. One member of this family, Liza Novikova, was my childhood friend. But when we grew up our paths parted: I went to a monastery and she, having finished theological school in the town of Kashir in the Tula province, became a school teacher in a village. Once in a while we would correspond; she was a kind, cheerful girl. Then the terrible time of trouble came to Russia: the red beast came. I lost all my friends because I lived a long distance from my homeland. But once I received a letter from Russia and, opening it up, I saw that it was from Liza Novikova, who was informing me of the death of her mother. Of course, I at once understood that Liza was no longer that believing girl I had known, that she had already infected her soul with unbelief in God. She wrote to me that, although the funeral had been conducted in church, she had not visited a temple in a long, long time and that "science is conquering all." Then she wrote to me a long letter, not hiding anything from me.

But still the last words of a communist girl touched me to the depth of my soul. She wrote to me: "Dear Misha (that was my worldly name), I've known you for a long time. I know that you are a religious man, that you believe in God and the immortality of the soul. And I ask you, Misha: pray for my mother — after all, she loved you and used to scold us that we seldom write to you. . . ." The letter was stained with tears. Then suddenly last year, 1936, during Great Lent, Liza Novikova came to my mind and for three days or so would not leave it. I wrote thus in a letter to Russia: "For such a long time now I haven't received a letter from Liza Novikova. Where does she live? Please inform me." And what would you think? I received a letter, and they wrote to me: "Apparently your soul felt something: Liza Novikova, having been sick for a week, died during Great Lent."

Here again she let me know with her soul that something had happened to her.

5.

Once I wrote a letter to Russia to one of my friends, an old lady who was very pious and God-loving. Here is what she wrote to me in her reply to my letter:

Dear Fr. Gerasim! I am very glad that you remembered me by writing me a letter. But I must tell you that I was expecting your letter, because Dounia came to me (that was her niece, the daughter of her sister) and said, "Auntie Luba! I saw my mother (who was dead) in my dream and she told me: 'Tell Luba that Fr. Gerasim has sent her a letter from America.'"

What actually is this? Does not this diary of events speak for the fact that our souls are immortal, that they are alive, that they abide in another world, in the Abodes of our Heavenly Father?

Here are two more cases of when I was informed by the dead of their unfortunate demise:

In 1908 I was working in the monastery infirmary. One July morning, about 2:00 a.m., I saw in my dream one of my acquaintances, who misused alcoholic beverages. I saw some dark place, where a crowd of black people were dragging my friend. His face was also black — only his white teeth were chattering as from a frightful cold. That black crowd, it seemed, was rejoicing and dancing. It quickly dragged the unfortunate one somewhere. I awoke out of fear: it was exactly 2:00 a.m., the bell was tolling for nocturnes. I crossed myself and wondered if the poor man had died from drunkenness. But in August of the same year, the wife of his brother visited me, and, giving all the news, asked me, "Did you hear that Andrey Ivanovich died?" "Yes," I answered, "they wrote to me about it." Then she looked at me with a piercing eye and, seeing my calm face, asked me again, "But did you hear how he died?" "No," I replied, "they did not write to me how." "The poor man committed suicide: he hung himself," she said. And then I told her my dream. When I told her when I had seen him, that it had been two o'clock in the morning, then she almost screamed: "Hold it, hold it, Misha! That's exactly when it occurred that night — early in the morning."

That autumn I visited his wife in the town of Alexin, and she told me everything in detail about his unfortunate death. It was absolutely true that he killed himself early in the morning in the month of July.

And here is a second case:

In St. Tikhon's Monastery I had a good friend, Monk Innocent. He was a humble man, kind, but he drank a lot. And although he was well educated, he was not ordained to a priestly rank because of his weakness for alcohol. In 1912, while living on Mount Athos, I saw in a dream that a crowd of black monsters were dragging Fr. Innocent all bound in chains and were beating him hard with sticks. From his face I could see that he suffered a lot. He tried to tell me something, but that black crowd did not give him a chance and quickly dragged him away.

When I returned to Russia in the fall of 1912, Monk Tryphon visited me in Tula, and we began to recollect our old friends. And when I told him about the dream I had seen on Mount Athos about Fr. Innocent, he told me, crying out: "Dear Misha, you must pray for him. That poor man died without repentance — he had a stroke."

And again, does this not speak for the fact that there is eternal life and that, according to the Word of God, for some it is joyful in our Heavenly Father's Mansions, and for others — for all unrepentant sinners — it is eternal suffering, since even the ancient prophet has said that *frightful is the death of the sinner.*

Having worked three years in the monastery infirmary and having spent twenty years in a parish in Alaska, I saw how both believing and unbelieving people die. And I tell you the truth: blessed indeed, thrice blessed, is the death of a believer!

I remember how in St. Tikhon's Monastery Fr. Jerome was dying. On his very last day all he said was that at four o'clock he would pass away. At 4:00 p.m. they struck the monastery bell for vespers, and the soul of Fr. Jerome quietly, accompanied by the pealing of the bell, flew away into eternity.

I also remember the death of Hiero-schemamonk Joseph who, sitting in an armchair, listened to the reading of the canon for the departure of the soul from the body. After the canon was completed, he quietly fell asleep in the sleep of the righteous forever. I remember the death of a young monk, Fr. Seraphim, who was dying even cheerfully while singing the Paschal canon.

And here is an exemplary death of an old lady in the village of Afognak in Alaska, Juliana Derenova. She lived until ripe old age and very much loved to go to the temple of God. When she felt her death approaching, she called me, had Confession, partook of Holy Communion and then with a trembling hand handed me a dollar. "Send this to the Lord's Sepulchre," she said, and then quietly, peacefully breathed her last. There were many such examples in this land, which is severe in its nature.

This truthful writing I will end with the words of a prayer to the Protectress of this cold world of ours:

Most Holy Mother of God, save us! Be the Preserver of our lives, O Most Holy One! Deliver us from the demons at the hour of our death, and after death be Thou our peace. Amen.

Archimandrite Gerasim Schmaltz
New Valaam, Spruce Island, Alaska
January, 1938

Translated from Khleb Nebesny, *Harbin, 1938, no. 11, pp. 14-17.*

Above: St. Michael's Skete of New Valaam Monastery, Spruce Island, Alaska, as it looks today.

At left: the new church of the St. Herman of Alaska Monastery in Platina, California, modelled after the Old Valaam church built by Abbot Nazarius during the time of St. Herman, 1793.

Epilogue
New Valaam Today

THE ST. HERMAN OF ALASKA BROTHERHOOD was born on New Valaam, Spruce Island. It was there, in 1961, that St. Herman gave a miraculous sign to one of the founding members, revealing that he would help in the establishment of a brotherhood in his name, and would send another brother — who turned out to be Fr. Seraphim Rose.

When the Brotherhood was formally established in San Francisco in 1963, Fr. Gerasim continually wrote from Spruce Island to ask about its progress. Despite his poverty, he sent the Brotherhood its first donation — a check for $25, and it was with this money, sent straight from Spruce Island, that the Brotherhood opened its bank account.

Fr. Gerasim hoped that the Brotherhood would not only help to bring about the universal glorification of St. Herman (who was then not yet canonized), but would also keep monasticism alive on Spruce Island. Already in advanced age and nearing death, he begged the brothers to "keep the monastic lamp burning" on St. Herman's New Valaam. At this time it was unfeasible for the brothers to move to the island. They felt that they first had to support themselves in the Northern California wilds by publishing and selling books, thereby setting up a monastic-missionary base from where "expansion" to Alaska might be possible. While the brothers kept the dream of New Valaam in their hearts, Fr. Gerasim

The original group of brothers who came from the St. Herman Monastery to New Valaam. At right is the Brotherhood's friend and benefactor, Nicholas Pestrikoff.

kept praying for the fulfillment of St. Herman's express wish for the formation of a monastery on the island. Only a month before Fr. Gerasim's repose in 1969, monastic life sprung up in the wilderness of Platina, California, as a preparation for New Valaam.

In 1982 Fr. Seraphim Rose, having served twenty years of incredible fruitfulness in the Brotherhood, was also approaching death. "You're dying now," his partner Abbot Herman told him. "But what about our obligations to Fr. Gerasim in Alaska? Bless us to go there now!" Tied to his hospital bed and unable to speak, Fr. Seraphim put all his effort into making the sign of the cross, blessing the move to Alaska.

The following Pascha, Fr. Herman went to Spruce Island to pray about the revival of New Valaam. And then, in August of 1983, less than a year after Fr. Seraphim's repose, seven brothers from the St. Herman Monastery in California departed for Alaska. Even as they kissed the holy shore of New Valaam, they were not sure of what the future would have in store for them: whether God and St. Herman would bless their desire, whether they would face obstacles from church authorities as Fr. Gerasim had, how the local people would react, and how they themselves would survive the severe northern nature. Obstacles and hindrances were indeed ahead of them, but soon they came to realize that such was the lot of all monastics who strove to follow in the footsteps of their much-suffering predecessors on the island.

In the midst of tribulations, however, came blessings. An Orthodox laywoman named Anna Opheim, who lived closer than anyone to St. Herman's home on the island, came to the rescue. She had been very close to Fr. Gerasim and loved him dearly. In her own way she knew what he stood for, and she wanted to keep his spirit alive. Had it not been for the help of Anna and her large family, the brothers would most likely not have been able to stay. It so happened that she and her husband Edward owned a large homestead. Since the rest of the island was owned by a recently-established "Native Corporation," this homestead was the only place where newcomers could legally settle.

It was on Fr. Gerasim's nameday in the world that the brothers hiked to the Opheims' home and were offered to buy a plot of land. Anna picked it out herself: an area with a hill overlooking the ocean strait and Mount Monashka ("Mount Nun") on the opposite shore. The view from the top was breathtaking. "I always felt that this spot was meant for something special," Anna said.

The next few years were occupied with building. The new edifice of New Valaam Monastery was called St. Michael's Skete, since it had been on St. Michael's Day that the Brotherhood had found the land. The construction of it proved rather difficult: the materials had to be hauled up the steep slope with pulleys and winches. But at last it was completed to the glory of God, and Fr. Gerasim's fervent prayers finally resulted in a veritable monastic citadel towering over Spruce Island.

So far it seems that St. Herman has blessed the renewed monastic presence at New Valaam. Since the Brotherhood's arrival in 1983 to the time of the present writing, there has been an unbroken monastic presence on the island. Sometimes there have been monks

Fr. Gerasim with Anna and Edward Opheim beside the Sts. Sergius and Herman church, 1940's.

The cross erected in memory of Anna Opheim on the hill of St. Michael's Skete. Anna died on the 150th anniversary of St. Herman's repose (Nov. 15/28, 1986).

Monks and nuns at the garden of New Valaam.
Photograph taken in September, 1988.

and sometimes nuns, but never has the island been devoid of monastics and the daily cycle of services. New Valaam Monastery follows the typicon of Old Valaam in Russia, beginning at 2:30 a.m. with the service of Nocturnes. The monastery is largely self-sufficient, living — as St. Herman did — on food it gathers from the earth and sea: fish, mushrooms, berries, and wild and cultivated vegetables.

Spruce Island is remarkably similar to the Russian island of Old Valaam: the same mossy forests, bright foliage and rocky cliffs. It is no wonder that St. Herman called his Alaskan home "New Valaam." Living there, one feels linked to the tradition and holiness which St. Herman brought from Valaam to America. Although New Valaam is but a small and humble monastic attempt, its inhabitants daily cherish the opportunity to be on these sacred grounds, "keeping the monastic lamp burning" according to the pious wish of their beloved father in the Lord, Archimandrite Gerasim.†

R. Monk Damascene
November, 1989

ARCHIMANDRITE GERASIM
Summer, 1960.